General and Flag Officer Costs

Annual Cost Estimates for General and Flag Officers
and Supporting Personnel

DAVID KNAPP, MICHAEL VASSEUR, HANNAH ACHESON-FIELD,
JONATHAN WELCH, LISA M. HARRINGTON

Prepared for the Office of the Secretary of Defense
Approved for public release; distribution unlimited

For more information on this publication, visit www.rand.org/t/RR4286

Library of Congress Cataloging-in-Publication Data is available for this publication.
ISBN: 978-1-9774-0423-7

Published by the RAND Corporation, Santa Monica, Calif.
© Copyright 2020 RAND Corporation
RAND® is a registered trademark.

Support RAND
Make a tax-deductible charitable contribution at
www.rand.org/giving/contribute

www.rand.org

Preface

This report provides cost estimates for direct and indirect costs associated with general and flag officers (G/FOs) generally and for specific positions in support of the Secretary of Defense's congressional reporting requirement as required by section 596 of the 2019 National Defense Authorization Act (NDAA). RAND Corporation researchers developed a framework for calculating direct and indirect costs associated with G/FOs. The framework uses existing administrative data where possible to facilitate future cost calculation while remaining consistent with the NDAA and the recommendations of the December 2017 report *Defining General and Flag Officer Costs* by the Office of Cost Assessment and Program Evaluation within the Office of the Secretary of Defense.

Our analysis took place between November 2018 and September 2019 and required collaboration with and support from offices across the U.S. Department of Defense (DoD), the services, and the Joint Staff. Cost estimates reflect assigned G/FO positions at the end of fiscal year 2018. Future costs will change as assigned G/FO positions and mission demands change. This report is intended for a broad audience but was written for Congress and readers with a general background on DoD personnel and manpower management issues.

This research was sponsored by the Office of Military Personnel Policy and conducted within the Forces and Resources Policy Center of the RAND National Defense Research Institute, a federally funded research and development center sponsored by the Office of the Secretary of Defense, the Joint Staff, the Unified Combatant Commands, the Navy, the Marine Corps, the defense agencies, and the defense Intelligence Community.

For more information on the RAND Forces and Resources Policy Center, see www.rand.org/nsrd/ndri/centers/frp or contact the director (contact information is provided on the webpage).

Contents

Tables

Summary

In this report, we document a framework for estimating the costs of general and flag officers (G/FOs) and their support personnel and use it to estimate these costs for fiscal year (FY) 2018. This cost-estimating framework is consistent with the requirements of section 596 of the 2019 National Defense Authorization Act (NDAA) (Pub. L. 115-232, 2018). The cost elements used in this framework are defined in the December 2017 report *Defining General and Flag Officer Costs* by the Office of Cost Assessment and Program Evaluation (CAPE) within the Office of the Secretary of Defense (Office of the Secretary of Defense, CAPE, 2017b). The framework is based on existing administrative data where possible to facilitate future cost estimates.

We estimate average annual total costs of typical G/FO positions as well as the annual total costs of specific G/FO positions. Typical G/FO cost estimates reflect the average of military officer positions with pay grades O-7 to O-10. Specific G/FO costs pertain to a unique position or a group of G/FOs with common mission characteristics (e.g., same functional area or command type). When estimating the cost of typical G/FO positions, we consider direct costs (e.g., direct compensation, deferred compensation, benefits) of a G/FO, his or her support personnel, and his or her training costs using CAPE's Full Cost of Manpower (FCoM) model. When estimating position-specific costs, we include these same cost elements, as well as position-specific allowances, average annual travel costs of G/FO serving in those positions and their support personnel who travel with them, the average cost of the G/FO quarters if the cost of those quarters consistently exceeds the basic allowance for housing to which they are entitled, and the cost of personal security details for those positions receiving continuous security. Prior to summarizing typical and specific cost estimates for G/FO positions, we highlight key limitations and note appropriate interpretation and use of these cost estimates.

Reported cost estimates depend on the quality and consistency of data collected, which varied by cost element. We identified three fundamental limitations in estimating costs of G/FO positions consistent with section 596 of the 2019 National Defense Authorization Act. First, the existing data systems that were accessible were unable to directly link a person to an authorized position. This limited the association of travel costs (which are person-specific) to a specific position. Second, existing data systems for tracking authorized positions vary across the services and joint-duty assignments, making it difficult to categorize support staff positions and associate them with a specific G/FO position. Finally, existing data systems are subject to user input error, which limited our ability to identify whether positions were authorized and filled. As detailed in this report, we tried to address these limitations by developing consistent approaches for categorizing support staff and for linking personnel with positions. However, these fixes were incomplete, and we noted where these limitations might result in over- or underestimated costs. We made several recommendations aimed at improving the accuracy and comparability of these cost estimates should the costing of G/FO positions be repeated, and we urge caution when making comparisons across services or with joint positions. Differences in cost could reflect inconsistency in reporting by organization or the data collected.

Reflecting the congressional request, the cost estimates in this report are total costs of G/FO positions that were filled by G/FOs at the end of FY 2018. Over time, if these cost estimates are repeatedly produced, they could be used to assess trends in overall G/FO costs as well as specific cost elements. An alternative measure to total cost is marginal cost. A *marginal cost* measures the change in total cost as a result of a change in a factor that contributes to the cost. Marginal costs are used for comparative purposes and are often more appropriate measures in policy analysis—for example, whether the policy under consideration is the cost savings associated with changing the authorized rank of a G/FO position or converting a position authorized for a G/FO to a civilian-equivalent authorization. More broadly, any policy analysis should also incorporate benefits of having a position filled by a G/FO, which is a factor not measured in this report.

When using the cost estimates provided in this report, it is important to note that G/FO positions vary in several key characteristics, including location, nature of position, organizational type, and function. Understanding the differences in positional characteristics and data quality associated with a G/FO position's cost estimates is necessary and should be documented when using G/FO cost estimates in an analysis or reporting them in a publication.

Table S.1 reports support staff averages by G/FO pay grade based on a consistent categorization and affiliation applied to documents of authorized positions provided by the services and Defense Manpower Data Center. Applying the cost-estimating framework, Table S.2 reports average annual total cost estimates by grade. Average annual total costs of typical G/FOs and their support staff increase with G/FO rank. The cost increase primarily reflects an increase in positional support (i.e., personnel that support the G/FO's mission), and there is a smaller increase in costs because of personal support (i.e., personnel that support the G/FO's personal needs). Training costs, as represented by FCoM, are constant within a military service and represent less than 2 percent of the typical G/FO costs.

Table S.1
Typical G/FO Average Support by Grade, All Services

Grade	Aide-de-Camp	Enlisted Aide	Other Personal	Executive Officer	Civilian Administrative Assistant	Enlisted Executive Assistant	Protocol	CAG	Overall
O-7	0.2	0.1	0.1	0.4	0.5	0.4	0.2	0.2	2.1
O-8	0.4	0.1	0.2	0.5	0.6	0.5	0.4	0.4	3.1
O-9	0.4	0.6	0.2	1.1	0.7	0.6	0.7	0.7	5.0
O-10	0.9	2.1	0.4	1.8	0.6	1.9	3.9	3.0	14.7

NOTES: Estimated values use manning documents provided for this study reflecting end of FY 2018. Sample sizes are reported in Table 2.4. This table reflects averages across all services based on these manning documents and applying a common support staff categorization with adjustments for consistency because of differences in service's or joint organizations' respective manning document terminology and structure. CAG = commander's action group.

Table S.2
Average Annual Total Costs (in Thousands) for a Typical G/FO

Grade	G/FO Direct Costs	Staff Direct Costs Personal	Staff Direct Costs Positional	G/FO Training (FCoM)	Total
O-7	$286	$64	$242	$5	$598
O-8	$321	$111	$362	$6	$799
O-9	$336	$198	$645	$5	$1,184
O-10	$336	$559	$2,071	$5	$2,971

NOTES: All costs expressed in 2018 dollars. Costs estimated using FCoM based on assumptions stated in Chapter Two of this report. Training is derived from the FCoM estimate and is not G/FO specific. Uses Washington, D.C., as the location for circumstances in which duty location could not be determined. Direct costs do not include position-specific allowances. Sample sizes are reported in Table 2.4.

In this report, we document that costs of specific G/FO positions vary substantially by nature of position, organizational type, and functional area. Estimated costs range from $270,000 annually for G/FOs in pay grade O-7 with no support personnel to more than $10 million annually for G/FOs in pay grade O-10 who receive continuous protection and are required to use government aircraft for official travel (e.g., service chiefs). High G/FO cost estimates are primarily driven by the direct costs of supporting personnel, including continuous security details and the cost of military air travel for personnel required to use it.

G/FO matters remain of great interest to Congress and are given routine attention in annual NDAAs. In anticipation that G/FO costs are estimated again in the future, we make nine recommendations aimed at improving and facilitating the estimation of G/FO costs. These recommendations apply only if G/FO costs are to be estimated in the future. The first five recommendations pertain to potential improvements in the G/FO costing definitions as approved in section 596 of the 2019 NDAA that would speed future estimation and improve the utility of G/FO costs estimates for policy analysis. The last four recommendations pertain to potential improvements that would facilitate data collection that could improve the accuracy of G/FO cost estimates.

Acknowledgments

We would like to thank Bill Atkinson, Special Assistant for Senior Officer Matters, Office of the Undersecretary of Defense for Personnel and Readiness (OUSD-P&R), and Garrett Summers, Office of Cost Analysis and Program Evaluation (CAPE) for their insights, comments, and support during this study. At the RAND Corporation, we appreciated the depth of knowledge provided by Bart Bennett about G/FO matters and the research support of Liam McLane. We also appreciate the leaders and staff in the service and joint senior leader management offices, manpower and personnel management offices, and other offices within the U.S. Department of Defense (DoD) who provided background, information, and feedback throughout the process, including BG T. J. Edwards, Leah Reid, and Matt Gillespie from the Army General Officer Management Office (GOMO); Col Colin Connor and Mary Morfitt from the U.S. Air Force GOMO; Brett Genoble and David Dillensnyder from Navy Flag Officer Management, Distribution and Development; Maj Gen David Ottignon, Michael Strobl, Lt Col Robyn Mestemacher, and Capt Alice Marcelo from Marine Corps Manpower Management Division; COL Elizabeth Griffin, COL Char Stallworth, Arthur Stovall, and LTC Thomas Manion from the Office of General/ Flag Officer Matters, Joint Staff; Erik Footland, Bill Kuhn, and My-Ly Andrews at the Defense Management Travel Office; Scott Seggerman, Ryan Czirban, and Terri Reisenfeld from the Defense Manpower Data Center; Curt Smolinsky, Cheryl Black, and Don Crutchfield from OUSD-P&R; Amanda Ritzman from CAPE; Melanie Valade from Canvas Management Associates; Harish Harihara Subramanian from the Army 21st Signal Brigade; Alicia Litts from the DoD comptroller; COL Tony Scott and CDR Ryan Carmichael from Joint Operational Support Airlift Center; Celia Gallo from Army Criminal Investigation Division; William Thomas, Gary Smith, and David Brown from the Naval Criminal Investigative Service; Col James Mehta, LtCol Trey Mamula, and Donovan Muir from the Air Force Office of Special Investigations; Bonnie Swanson from the National Defense University; Christopher Rizzo from the Army War College; James Zummeren from the Lejeune Leadership Institute at Marine Corps University; Eric Dauer from the Marine Corps Housing Program; Marlow Gogel from U.S. Air Force Housing, Asset Management Division; Stephen Drumm from the Navy Housing Programming & Resource Manager (N93); Matthew Conlan from Army Housing Division; Heather Jackson from Headquarters, Department of the Army (HQDA), G1; Curtis Million from HQDA, G3/5/7; George Meehan from Total Force Structure Division, Combat Development and Integration; and Elsy-Rose Brazil from Headquarters Marine Corps. Our research benefited from the review of Jennifer Lamping-Lewis at RAND, and our report benefited from helpful comments and input by Ellen Pint at RAND and Edward Keating at the Congressional Budget Office.

Abbreviations

AF/A1	Office of the Deputy Chief of Staff of the Air Force for Personnel
AFSC	Air Force Specialty Code
BAH	basic allowance for housing
BAS	basic allowance for subsistence
BSC	Billet Sequence Code
CAG	commander's action group
CAPE	Cost Analysis and Program Evaluation
CD&I	Capabilities development/integration
CJCS	Chairman of the Joint Chiefs of Staff
CSAF	Chief of Staff of the Air Force
C4I	command, control, communications, computers, and intelligence
DEPTID	department identification code
DMDC	Defense Manpower Data Center
DoD	U.S. Department of Defense
DoDI	Department of Defense Instruction
DoDIG	Department of Defense Inspector General
DTMO	Defense Travel Management Office
DTS	Defense Travel System
FAC	functional area code

FCoM	Full Cost of Manpower
FMET	force management, development, education, and training
FO	flag officer
FY	fiscal year
GAO	U.S. Government Accountability Office
G/FO	general and flag officer
GO	general officer
GOMO	General Officer Management Office
GS	general schedule
HRP	high-risk personnel
JOSAC	Joint Operational Support Airlift Center
MERHC	Medicare-Eligible Retiree Health Care
MILAIR	military air transport
MILPER	military personnel
NATO	North Atlantic Treaty Organization
NDAA	National Defense Authorization Act
NDU	National Defense University
OFFICEID	office identifier combination
ORF	official representation funds
OSC	office symbol code
OSD	Office of the Secretary of Defense
OHA	overseas housing allowance
OPM	Office of Personnel Management
O&M	operations and maintenance
PARNO	paragraph number
PCS	permanent change of station

PEO/PPO	Program Executive Officer/protection-providing organization
PSD	personal security detail
R&D	research and development
UIC	unit identification code
USFK	U.S. Forces Korea
USFOR-A	U.S. Forces—Afghanistan
VA	Veterans Affairs

CHAPTER ONE

Introduction

This report provides estimates of general and flag officer (G/FO) annual costs consistent with section 596 the 2019 National Defense Authorization Act (NDAA) (Pub. L. 115-232, 2018). The 2019 NDAA stated that these estimates were to reflect direct and indirect costs associated with typical G/FOs as well as estimates for specific positions. Furthermore, these estimates were to reflect the recommendations of the December 2017 report *Defining General and Flag Officer Costs* published by the Office of the Secretary of Defense's (OSD's) Office of Cost Assessment and Program Evaluation (CAPE) (OSD, CAPE, 2017b).[1]

The CAPE report addressed an earlier congressional requirement from the 2016 NDAA to define costs associated with G/FOs, their staff and aides, and costs associated with their work, such as security details and travel (Pub. L. 114-92, 2015). CAPE's report provided recommendations for what costs to include but did not provide cost estimates. CAPE's recommendations were broadly accepted in section 596 of the 2019 NDAA, with the exception that Congress required the cost estimates to consider costs associated with the upkeep and maintenance of official residences not captured by the basic allowance for housing (BAH) and, on a case-by-case basis, costs associated with enlisted and officer aide travel, taking into consideration the cost of data collection.

Scope and Key Limitations

This study estimates costs for G/FOs within the four military services in the U.S. Department of Defense (DoD). G/FOs are defined as service members with pay grades O-7 to O-10 (see Table 1.1). They will be referred to by their pay grade throughout this report.

OSD, CAPE (2017b) defined G/FO cost elements. It did not collect the required data to estimate G/FO costs and did not identify all G/FO positions. Additionally, although the 2019 NDAA required estimates for specific positions, it neither stated the positions nor the period to be considered. Consequently, in consultation with the

---

[1] These recommendations are detailed and discussed in Chapter Two.

Table 1.1
G/FO Grades, Ranks, and Insignia

Pay Grade	Insignia	Air Force Rank	Army Rank	Marine Corps Rank	Navy Rank
O-10	★★★★	General	General	General	Admiral
O-9	★★★	Lieutenant General	Lieutenant General	Lieutenant General	Vice Admiral
O-8	★★	Major General	Major General	Major General	Rear Admiral
O-7	★	Brigadier General	Brigadier General	Brigadier General	Rear Admiral (Lower Half)

study's sponsor, we limited the scope of the study to active-duty G/FO authorizations that were filled by G/FOs as of the end of fiscal year (FY) 2018, and we estimated annual costs for FY 2018.[2]

We detail other decisions regarding scope throughout the report. Examples of additional decisions regarding scope include the period to consider for travel costs and the costs of official residences, as these costs can vary substantially from year to year. Additionally, although the CAPE report provided general details regarding cost elements, it did not attempt to identify specific G/FOs, consistently categorize support staff, link support staff to specific G/FOs, or specify various other required steps to estimate the costs as defined.

Next, we introduce background on studies related to G/FO matters, including previous congressionally requested reports that have led to this study. Then we introduce how different types of cost estimates can be used and interpreted. We conclude the introduction by reviewing the research approach and outlining the report. In the next chapter, we detail our cost estimation framework and discuss cost definitions recommended in OSD, CAPE (2017b).[3]

Previous Studies on G/FO Matters

Two related issues pertaining to G/FOs receive regular interest from Congress. The first is the total number of personnel allowed to hold a specific G/FO rank across the services and in joint organizations as authorized by Congress. The services and the Chairman of the Joint Chiefs of Staff (CJCS) establish the need for positions

---

[2]   We define an *authorization* as a position that is designated to be filled with a G/FO, either by the services or by a joint organization.

[3]   Throughout the report, we use *framework* instead of *methodology* to emphasize that we are identifying guidelines that are meant to maintain a common set of principles (i.e., the cost definitions) but that are flexible enough to allow for differences based on data available by cost element or data available across services.

to be designated for a G/FO and then authorize for the position to be filled up to limits set by Congress. Congress requested that DoD conduct a study of its G/FO requirements in 1966, and that request has been repeated at regular intervals since that time (Offenhauer, 2007). The number of G/FOs has varied substantially since 2000. In May 2019, there were 906 G/FOs on active duty across the U.S. Army, U.S. Navy, U.S. Marine Corps, and U.S. Air Force. This is less than the 981 G/FOs on active duty in September 2010 but more than the 871 G/FOs in September 2001 (Defense Manpower Data Center [DMDC], various dates).[4]

The 2017 NDAA reduced G/FO authorizations by 110, with implementation to be completed by December 31, 2022. Additionally, it directed the Secretary of Defense to conduct a comprehensive study of requirements for G/FOs with a goal of identifying an additional 10-percent reduction in G/FO authorizations. Harrington et al. (2018) developed a methodology to assess active-component G/FO requirements and authorizations and applied that methodology to identify opportunities to eliminate, downgrade, or convert G/FO positions to civilian positions.

The second issue receiving regular interest by Congress is G/FO costs, including direct compensation and indirect costs. Two recent reports in response to NDAA requests (GAO, 2014; OSD, CAPE, 2017b) address G/FO costs directly. Beyond these reports, interest in G/FO costs has narrowly focused on specific costs, including official residences, aides (officer and enlisted), and official representation funds (ORF).[5] We briefly review GAO (2014) and the OSD, CAPE report (2017b), then discuss other applicable streams of congressional oversight that may influence G/FO cost estimates or the use and interpretation of cost estimates.

GAO and OSD, CAPE G/FO Cost Reports
Based on congressional requests in 2013, GAO conducted the first recent comprehensive review of the cost of G/FOs as a distinct group from other service members (GAO, 2014). The study was conducted for three main reasons: to look for cost savings in a particularly challenging fiscal environment, to address why DoD was not satisfactorily updating Congress on its changes in G/FO requirements, and to address a perception of G/FO financial misconduct. GAO examined trends in costs of active-duty G/FOs from FY 2001 to FY 2013 and considered costs from a federal perspective. It defined

---

[4] The U.S. Government Accountability Office (GAO) (2014) provides a more extensive discussion of trends in the number of G/FOs relative to non-G/FOs and enlisted personnel. Note that, prior to 2004, what is currently known as the U.S. Government Accountability Office was called the U.S. *General Accounting* Office. In this report, we use the abbreviation *GAO* when referring to the post-2004 name of the office and write out "U.S. General Accounting Office" when referring to the pre-2004 name.

[5] ORF are appropriated funds used to host official events and extend courtesies to guests of the United States and DoD to maintain their respective standing and prestige. These events are normally hosted and attended by members of the senior executive service and G/FOs (Department of Defense Instruction [DoDI] 7250.13, 2017).

the scope of expenses that should be included when accounting the cost of G/FOs, including

- compensation[6]
- tax expenditure[7]
- housing costs
- health care costs
- commercial travel and per diem
- military and government air travel
- official representation costs
- executive training costs
- security details
- aide compensation
- aide travel and per diem
- aide housing costs.

When GAO attempted to identify and estimate these costs, they encountered inconsistency in data quality and availability. Of the categories just listed, complete data were only available for G/FO compensation, tax expenditure, housing costs, health care costs, commercial travel and per diem, and executive training as of 2013.

GAO (2014) recommended that the Secretary of Defense publish guidance on both enlisted and officer aide reporting, formally define officer aide positions, and require reporting on officer aide positions. Finally, GAO also recommended in its report that CAPE "define costs that could be associated with G/FOs."

Reflecting these recommendations, the 2016 NDAA directed the Secretary of Defense to define costs that could be associated with G/FOs. OSD, CAPE (2017b) provided these cost definitions and furthered GAO's work by categorizing costs and providing recommendations on how to estimate them using data that could be feasibly collected from DoD organizations. The report recommended including most of the cost elements identified in GAO (2014). It did not recommend including some costs mentioned in that report, including

- special pay which it believed to be too sporadic
- ORF

---

[6] GAO (2014) noted that the compensation costs reflected DoD's composite standard pay rates. The report stated that these rates are "used by DOD when determining the military personnel appropriations cost for budget and management studies" and include "average basic pay plus retired pay accrual, Medicare-eligible retiree health care accrual; basic allowances for housing and subsistence; incentive, miscellaneous, and special pays; and permanent change of station expenses" (GAO, 2014, pp. 4, 27).

[7] GAO (2014, p. 19) defines *tax expenditure* as "the tax revenue forgone by the federal government by the policy of not taxing the basic allowance for housing and the basic allowance for subsistence."

- official residences, which it believed BAH already captured.

OSD, CAPE (2017b) emphasized the use of their Full Cost of Manpower (FCoM) model where possible, including the estimation of direct and deferred compensation and health care costs for G/FOs, as well as these costs for support personnel.[8] It also recommended using the aggregate, pay grade–neutral costs of training from FCoM, which differ from the G/FO-specific executive training costs collected in GAO (2014).

OSD, CAPE (2017b) highlighted the differences between positional costs and those associated with rank. This motivated separate cost elements being included when evaluating specific G/FO positions. Perhaps most important, it devised a repeatable framework. It did not go so far as to calculate the costs of particular positions, but it clarified what costs should be included for all G/FOs and for specific G/FO positions.

Additional Research on Manpower and G/FO Costs

Congressional, GAO, and DoD research on military compensation has considered military compensation broadly (not targeted at G/FOs). One of the key aspects of military service is that service members enter at a low rank and are developed and promoted from within their service. The military has no lateral entry. Rosen (1992) notes that promotion and compensation must be adequately set to retain a sufficient number of qualified individuals to support the military hierarchy and motivate personnel at each level of the organization. To understand whether compensation is sufficient to retain service members, studies will often attempt to identify service members' employment and earning options if they were to leave the military. For example, GAO (2010) compared pay and benefits of service members with comparable private-sector employees to assess how the differences in pay and benefits affect recruiting and retention of service members. This and related GAO studies and others have relied on regular military compensation to reflect direct compensation (e.g., GAO, 2014; Hosek et al., 2018). Regular military compensation reflects a service member's basic pay, tax-free allowances such as BAH, and basic allowance for subsistence (BAS), as well as the federal income tax advantage associated with those tax-free allowances. The incorporation of the federal income tax advantage reflects how much more a comparable civilian would have to be paid to receive the same level of posttax income. By choosing to compensate service members using tax-free allowances, DoD conceptually receives an intragovernment transfer from the U.S. Department of the Treasury via forgone tax revenues.

A related stream of congressional interest, conceptually distinct from military compensation, is in accounting of the FCoM. The focus in these studies is on the comparative cost of different workforces within DoD, such as the military, federal

---

[8]   FCoM is a cost-analysis tool designed to provide a consistent method for personnel and compensation analysis across DoD to calculate the FCoM as defined by CAPE and the OSD comptroller.

civilian employee, and civilian contractor workforces. Emphasis in these contexts has generally been on the full cost of personnel to the taxpayer, with the purpose being to understand the implications of those costs to DoD and the federal government when making policy decisions and programming commitments (GAO, 2013). The full-cost approach typically accounts for cost factors beyond direct compensation, including health care costs and the costs to recruit and train personnel. FCoM, the model used to estimate personnel costs in this study, was developed in response to the need for a DoD-wide recognized method of accounting for the FCoM. FCoM was designed with the total force in mind and not specifically for estimating the cost of G/FOs. This has implications for how we use cost estimates derived from FCoM. When applied to a specific type of analysis, some of the assumptions in FCoM may be incorrect, as the cost elements may change with pay grade in a way that is not well captured by FCoM (e.g., G/FO-specific training costs).

Neither of these streams of congressional interest have focused on the implications for G/FO position costs from the lack of lateral entry in the military or from changes in the nature of the military's hierarchy (e.g., the legislated reduction in G/FO personnel). The lack of lateral entry into the military means that, to maintain the quality of officers filling G/FO positions, promotion and compensation must be set to maintain officer quality (Rosen, 1992; Asch et al., 2016). The cost of a G/FO position could be defined to include the cost of maintaining quality leaders for filling these positions, which might then lead to the inclusion of personnel costs associated with recruiting, retaining, developing, and screening a cohort of junior officers to maintain that chosen level of quality. These costs are not fully reflected in the G/FO position costs estimated in this report. Changes to the structure of the military hierarchy also have implications for the cost of the G/FO positions that remain. If the military's mission and size is maintained but the number of G/FO positions is reduced, greater demands on the remaining G/FO positions may necessitate more support personnel to facilitate a G/FO's expanded mission. This may lead to greater costs associated with the remaining G/FO positions.

G/FO-Specific Personal Benefits and Support

In addition to manpower costs, Congress has demonstrated interest in benefits afforded primarily to G/FOs: official residences (or quarters), aides (both enlisted and officers), and ORF.

In 1999, the Navy and Air Force notified Congress that they had used operations and maintenance (O&M) funds to maintain official residences and exceeded the $25,000 cap per property per year (Office of the Inspector General, Department of Defense [DoDIG], 2000). This resulted in a review by DoDIG, which ultimately found that management controls of the O&M costs of G/FO quarters were adequate, but they were not fully implemented (DoDIG, 2000). The cost of specific official residences maintained by each service are now reported annually as part of each service's O&M

budget request,[9] and additional DoD guidance is provided in the latest version of the DoD Manual 4165.63, *DoD Housing Management* (2018).

G/FOs have access to several forms of personal support. The two main programs are enlisted aides and officer aides-de-camp. DoDI 1315.09 defines enlisted aides as "authorized for the purpose of relieving G/FOs of those minor tasks and details which, if performed by the G/FOs, would be at the expense of the G/FOs' primary military and other official duties and responsibilities" (DoDI 1315.09, 2017, p. 1). Currently, these authorizations are based on whether the official duties and responsibilities of the G/FO position merit enlisted aide support and are not solely dependent on grade or title of the G/FO (GAO, 2016). In December 1972, there were 1,722 enlisted aide authorizations supporting some 970 officers, mostly G/FOs but also more than 100 Navy captains (U.S. General Accounting Office, 1973). However, following the U.S. General Accounting Office's report (1973), DoD reduced the size of the enlisted aide program by 83 percent to only 300 total (U.S. General Accounting Office, 1973, 1983; GAO, 2016; 10 USC § 981). In 2019, there were 255 assigned enlisted aides.

Unlike enlisted aides, the roles for commissioned officer aides-de-camp are not as well defined. In a report on allegations of improper use of an aide-de-camp, DoDIG reviewed policies of the Joint Staff, Army, and the Air Force. DoDIG (2018) noted that the Joint Staff issued a "Quick Reference Guide," dated June 2017, that indicated officer aides "are assigned to enable the [flag officer (FO)] to perform their official duties more effectively." DoDIG (2018) noted that an officer aide's "office duties" may include "assistance in personal matters" for the general officer (GO). For the Air Force, DoDIG (2018) noted that the Air Force General Officer Management Office issued a "General Officer Handbook," dated 2017, which stated that an aide-de-camp's duties are "outlined in the Air Force Officer Classification Directory." That directory, dated October 31, 2016, stated that an officer aide "performs duties as assigned," and GAO (2014) emphasized the need to better categorize enlisted and officer aides, which was formalized as a biennial reporting requirement in the 2015 NDAA. However, officer aides continue to be inconsistently defined and tracked.

ORF are governed by DoDI 7250.13 (2017), which details who can approve the use of ORF, who can host an event funded by ORF, fees that are reimbursable with ORF, under what circumstances such an event may be hosted, and who may attend that event. Previously, ORF were not well defined or regulated. Following a 1982 article on the use of ORF, the U.S. General Accounting Office conducted an investigation (1982).[10] There have not been additional studies specific to ORF since that 1982 study.

---

[9] Reported for service-owned and privately leased quarters as part of the "General and Flag Officer Quarters" budget exhibit.

[10] The U.S. General Accounting Office (1982) found "that it was not clear how expenses not specifically addressed in [DoD] guidance should be charged or how much time can be spent on social activities peripherally related to official business." Consequently, the U.S. General Accounting Office recommended that the Secretary

However, misuse of ORF and travel funds have been identified as part of specific investigations (see, for example, Chandrasekaran and Jaffe, 2012).

Interpreting and Using G/FO Cost Estimates

Reflecting the congressional request in the 2019 NDAA, the G/FO cost estimates provided in this report are annual total costs of G/FO positions that are filled by a G/FO as of the end of FY 2018. Total cost estimates include the costs of holding a specific position regardless of rank. For example, a specific position might have a substantial number of qualifying representation events that result in the assignment of enlisted aides or protocol staff. Total costs also include rank-specific costs, such as basic pay; costs that reflect both rank and characteristics of a position, such as the location based BAH; and costs associated with the position's mission.

Total cost is one measurement of G/FO costs. Once a consistent methodology is developed, total costs can be estimated to evaluate trends in G/FO costs. An alternative measure is marginal cost, which measures the change in total cost because of a change in a factor that contributes to the cost. Marginal costs are used for comparative purposes. For example, suppose an analysis aims to measure the cost of changing the authorized rank associated with a G/FO position. The marginal cost of a rank change should reflect the implications of that change on the rank-associated cost elements, including the G/FO's direct compensation and G/FO support (e.g., assigned aides may have a lower rank and hence a lower cost). A marginal cost holds constant the cost of factors that do not change. In the rank-reduction example, constant factors would include location, nature of position, organizational type, and function that affect G/FO and G/FO support costs but are not directly influenced by a rank change.

The appropriate G/FO cost measure to use in an analysis or report depends on the purpose for using or reporting a G/FO cost estimate. Most often, cost estimates are used for comparative purposes (e.g., changing authorized rank of a G/FO position), in which case a marginal cost measure is most appropriate. The purpose for making a comparison is important because the purpose determines the appropriate comparison group, and the appropriate comparison group determines the appropriate measure.

The G/FO cost estimates provided in this report are annual total costs of G/FO positions and reflect characteristics of the G/FO position and the varying quality of data that are used to estimate costs. G/FO positions vary in several key characteristics, including location, nature of position, organizational type, and function. G/FO positions by service may also vary along these characteristics. As later detailed in Chapter Two, the data provided to identify and associate potential support staff with G/FOs varied

---

of Defense direct the military departments to follow the existing guidance more closely and update where insufficient. The applicable DoD instructions have been updated since.

by service. Although we tried to ensure comparable estimates, we documented various cases in which differences and inconsistencies in the data used for estimates might lead to under- or overestimated costs of one service relative to another. Throughout the report, we refer to differences in positional characteristics and data quality by service and joint organizations as *context*. Understanding the context associated with a G/FO position's cost estimates is necessary and should be documented when using G/FO cost estimates in an analysis or reporting them in a publication.

Study Approach and Organization of Report

In this study, we followed the cost definitions established in OSD, CAPE (2017b) and emphasized replicability of data collection and estimation in developing the cost-estimating framework. To do this, we collected data from each of the services regarding G/FO positions, including the manning documents for each G/FO office. Where possible, we relied on information extracted from existing manpower and personnel systems. Chapter Two documents our cost-estimating framework, including the specific cost categories required by Congress, definitions of those cost categories by OSD, CAPE (2017b), data sources, and limitations of the cost-estimating framework. The discussion of the limitations of the cost-estimating framework includes key methodological challenges, consequences of the limitations on G/FO cost estimates, and the implications for interpreting and using G/FO cost estimates. In Chapter Three, the cost of typical G/FOs are reported by pay grade and service or joint positions, and differences across services are discussed. Chapter Four reports costs of specific G/FO positions, with a focused discussion of two examples: the service chiefs and the CJCS, and brigadier generals in the Army by functional area, organization type, and nature of the position (additional specific cost estimates are included in Appendix A). Chapter Five provides a summary of G/FO cost estimates and revisits important limitations, as well as nine recommendations that apply if G/FO costs are to be estimated in the future.

CHAPTER TWO

General and Flag Officer Cost-Estimating Framework

In this chapter, we develop a framework that estimates costs associated with a G/FO typically and for specific positions. This framework includes

1. a delineation of included cost elements
2. a defined method for estimating each cost element
3. an approach for identifying specific G/FO positions filled as of the end FY 2018
4. an approach for categorizing G/FO support positions
5. an approach for associating cost elements with specific G/FO positions.

This framework is consistent with the requirements of section 596 of NDAA 2019 (Pub. L.115-232, 2018) and OSD, CAPE (2017b), including using the same framework and data sources as CAPE's 2018 FCoM model to calculate direct and indirect costs when possible.

In the first section, we introduce the G/FO cost categories enumerated in section 596 of the 2019 NDAA. Next, we define specific cost elements in each category and discuss how they are estimated, including the source of data used. We note any areas in which additional decisions or assumptions are made based on available data or other areas of ambiguity. We then discuss our approach to identifying G/FO positions and how support staff are categorized and associated with a specific G/FO position. We conclude by discussing key methodological challenges that are the result of available data and discuss the implications for our typical and position-specific G/FO cost estimates.

Required Cost Categories

Eleven cost categories, paraphrased in Table 2.1, were identified in the 2019 NDAA (Pub. L. 115-232, 2018).

Adopting the definitions in OSD, CAPE (2017b), the 2019 NDAA defined the cost of a typical G/FO position as including costs that are associated with a particular rank and service, regardless of position. These include direct cost categories, such as

Table 2.1
G/FO Cost Categories

NDAA Cost Category	Cost Group	Used in Typical[a] Analysis	Used in Position-Specific[a] Analysis
1. Direct compensation	G/FO direct costs	X	X
2. Personal money allowances	G/FO direct costs		X
3. Deferred compensation and health care costs	G/FO direct costs	X	X
4. Costs associated with providing security details for G/FO positions that merit continuous security	G/FO protection detail costs		X
5. Costs associated with government and commercial travel for G/FO positions qualifying for tier one or two travel	G/FO travel		X
6. G/FO per diem costs	G/FO travel		X
7. Costs for G/FO enlisted and officer aide housing	Staff direct costs	X	X
8. Costs associated with enlisted and officer aide travel	Staff travel		X
9. Costs associated with additional support staff for G/FOs and their travel, equipment, and per diem costs	Staff direct costs, staff travel	Direct costs only	X
10. Costs associated with the upkeep and maintenance of official residences not captured by basic housing assistance	G/FO official residences		X
11. Costs associated with training for G/FOs	G/FO training	X	X

NOTE: NDAA cost categories and assigned use in typical and position-specific analyses reflect section 596 of the 2019 NDAA (Pub. L. 115-232, 2018). Cost groups reflect the authors' grouping using data sources. Incorporating only direct costs for support personnel in the "typical" analysis is consistent with the exclusion of G/FO travel in typical analyses and reflects the authors' interpretation of likely intent using OSD, CAPE (2017b).

[a] Typical and position-specific analyses differ; that is, the typical G/FO cost estimates include costs associated with a particular rank and service, regardless of position. Position-specific G/FO cost estimates include all the costs from the typical estimates, plus several additional direct and indirect costs (e.g., personal money allowances as applicable by G/FO position, direct costs of security details for the subset of G/FO positions receiving continuous security protection).

direct and deferred compensation, and indirect cost categories, such as support staff costs and the cost of a G/FO's training.

The cost of a specific G/FO position includes the typical G/FO costs as well as costs associated with a particular position, independent of rank. This includes direct cost categories, such as personal money allowances, and indirect cost categories, such as protective details, travel, and official residences.

Some of the cost categories in Table 2.1 have overlapping estimation methods and data sources, while other cost categories require multiple data sources with differentiated estimation methods based on the data source. Table 2.1 assigns each cost category to a cost group that will be used in the next section when discussing estimation methods and data sources.

Cost Definitions, Methods, and Data Sources

Costs are split into the direct and indirect costs associated with a G/FO. Direct costs reflect annual expenses associated with employing a service member or civilian or providing benefits to them. Indirect costs reflect expenses related to a service member or civilian performing the duties associated with his or her position. Indirect costs include the direct costs of G/FO supporting personnel (including security details if required by the position), as well as the supporting personnel's travel incurred while supporting the G/FO. We distinguish among six different indirect G/FO cost groups:

- staff direct costs
- G/FO travel
- staff travel
- G/FO official residences
- G/FO training costs
- G/FO protection detail costs.

All values used in our analysis reflect those in effect at the end of FY 2018 unless otherwise noted (e.g., we use military and federal pay tables in effect on September 30, 2018).

In the next several subsections, we detail each cost group, including associated cost elements, how the costs are estimated, and the data sources used in estimating those costs. In this analysis, we identified ambiguities or limitations using data we collected that do not allow this analysis to exactly follow the recommendations in OSD, CAPE (2017b). In such instances, we note where additional decisions or assumptions are made and how they differ from recommendations in OSD, CAPE (2017b). One such instance is that FCoM cost estimates used in this report reflect those of the federal government, including costs to the military components, DoD, and non-DoD agencies of the federal government. Section 596 of the 2019 NDAA and OSD, CAPE (2017b) were not clear about whether G/FO costs should reflect costs to the federal government or only to DoD. This implementation is largely consistent with the notion of the FCoM reflecting the full cost of personnel to the taxpayer as described in GAO (2013), although it does not include forgone federal tax revenue from the policy of not taxing BAH and the BAS, as this is excluded from FCoM.

G/FO and Staff Direct Costs

Direct costs include compensation paid directly to an individual and DoD-incurred cost. We use all manpower costs reflected in FCoM, which are detailed in Table 2.2 for service members and Table 2.3 for civilians. Civilians are relevant in our analysis of G/FO costs insofar as they serve in supporting capacities to G/FOs.

Direct costs associated with a service member include their direct compensation in basic pay and allowances. Basic pay, which is set annually by Congress, is paid by the service component's annual military personnel (MILPER) budget and depends on rank and years of service. Service members located in the United States (excluding U.S. territories and possessions) receive BAH, which is paid by their component and reflects "equitable housing compensation based on housing costs in local civilian housing markets within the United States when government quarters are not provided" (Defense Travel Management Office [DTMO], 2019a). BAH depends on location, rank, and number of dependents. We assume all service members have dependents in our cost estimates, and, for our typical cost estimate, we assume G/FOs are based in the Washington, D.C., metro area for units where locations could not be identified. Service members living outside the United States (including U.S. territories and possessions) are eligible for an overseas housing allowance (OHA), which is paid to service members who must privately rent housing while stationed overseas and is intended to "partially defray housing costs when on-base or government leased housing is not available" (DTMO, 2019b). This includes the cost of utilities. OHA, such as BAH, depends on a service member's rank, location, and dependents. All service members receive a BAS that is meant to offset the cost of meals (DoD, undated-a). The amount varies between enlisted and officers but does not vary by rank within those categories. BAH, OHA, and BAS are not taxed. Direct compensation in FCoM does not include this tax advantage, which is a cost to the federal government in the form of forgone tax revenue from the U.S. Department of the Treasury. The tax advantage associated with these allowances is typically included when estimating regular military compensation to approximate an equivalent civilian salary (DoD, undated-b) and was used in earlier reviews of G/FO costs (see GAO, 2014). Although the estimates included in this report use FCoM because it is required by the 2019 NDAA, it would be logically consistent to include the tax advantage in future G/FO cost estimates if considering costs to the federal government. We recommend including the tax advantage in future G/FO cost estimates if the purpose of those estimates is to reflect the cost to the federal government or taxpayer.

Direct costs associated with a service member also include costs of fringe benefits, which are benefits not paid directly to the service member. These include payments for a service member's retirement, moves, health care, and insurance-related costs. To fund service members' retirement, a retired pay accrual charge is incurred by each component and is a fixed multiple of base pay. The charge reflects the amount required "to fully fund the retirement liability of entering cohorts of MILPER, taking into account the

Table 2.2
Military Direct Cost Elements

FCoM Manpower Cost Element	FCoM Data Source[a]	Government Organization Bearing Cost	Location Dependent	Rank Dependent	Years of Service Dependent	Service Dependent
Basic pay	Defense finance and accounting service	Component		X	X	
BAH or OHA	DTMO	Component	X	X		
BAS	OSD compensation	Component		E/O		
Retired pay accrual	OSD comptroller	Component		X	X	
Medicare-Eligible Retiree Health Care (MERHC)	OSD comptroller	Component				
Treasury contribution to MERHC fund	OPM annual budget documents	Federal government				
Health care	OSD comptroller: MILPER composite standard pay and reimbursement	DoD				
Permanent change of station (PCS)/relocation	Service comptroller (MILPERS)	Component		E/O		X
Education assistance	Service comptroller (O&M)	Component				X
Miscellaneous expenses	Service comptroller (MILPERS)	Component		X		X
Discount groceries	OSD comptroller: financial summary tables DoD budget	DoD				
Child development (day care facilities)	Service comptrollers (O&M)	DoD				

Table 2.2—Continued

FCoM Manpower Cost Element	FCoM Data Source[a]	Government Organization Bearing Cost	Location Dependent	Rank Dependent	Years of Service Dependent	Service Dependent
DoD education activity and family assistance	OSD comptroller (O&M)	DoD				
Child education (impact aid)	Department of Education impact aid annual budget request	Federal government				
Treasury contribution for concurrent receipts	OPM annual budget documents	Federal government				
Veterans benefits (cash and in-kind)	U.S. Department of Veterans Affairs (VA) annual budget submission	Federal government				
Training	Service comptrollers (O&M)	Component				X
Recruitment and advertising	Service comptrollers (O&M)	Component				X

NOTES: OPM = Office of Personnel Management. "Dependent" indicates whether a specific cost element is dependent on location, rank, years of service, or military service. For rank-dependent cost elements, the cost element may vary by each grade, in which case it is marked with an "X," and, in other cases, it depends only on the distinction of enlisted or commissioned officers, in which case it is marked "E/O." For service members, miscellaneous expenditures reflect MILPERS costs outside the other MILPERS cost categories. According to OSD, CAPE (2017a), "[m]iscellaneous costs include such things as: Overseas Station Allowance, Continental United States (CONUS) Cost-of-living allowance (COLA), clothing allowance, unemployment benefits, and a myriad of other things."
[a] Cost element or the information required to compute the cost element as described in the text can be found on the listed data provider's website.

expected growth in military pay, interest rates, and other factors such as mortality rates" (Hosek et al., 2017, pp. 1–2) and is set annually by the DoD Office of the Actuary. The rate of the retired pay accrual does not vary by component or rank. Each component is responsible for paying the MERHC accrual charges. Similar to the retired pay accrual charge, the MERHC accrual charge is intended to reflect the amount required to fully fund future retiree health care benefits and is a fixed rate regardless of rank or service. Separately, the U.S. Department of the Treasury contributes to the MERHC fund. MERHC accruals are paid by "permanent, indefinite appropriations from the General

Fund of the Treasury," however, MERHC accruals are counted as part of the military service's discretionary budget authority and so are included in the service's annual MILPERS budget requests (Tompkey, 2019). DoD pays for health benefits, and the OSD comptroller reports an annual reimbursement rate for medical health care costs of active-duty personnel and their dependents (Tompkey, 2019). FCoM reflects the retired pay accrual charge using base pay, the fixed MERHC accrual charge by both DoD and the Treasury, and the fixed annual reimbursement rate medical health care costs.

Costs associated with military-required relocations, known as PCS, are incorporated into FCoM by estimating an average relocation cost for officers and enlisted members by service. This value is computed by dividing the annual PCS travel budget for officers and enlisted members as reported in each service's MILPERS budget request by the service's active-duty end strength for officers and enlisted members. Education assistance includes funding for off-duty and voluntary education for the service member's personal or professional development. This value is computed by dividing the annual off-duty and voluntary education budget for service members as reported in each service's annual O&M budget request by the service's active-duty end strength. Using service MILPER budgets, FCoM further defines a category of miscellaneous personnel expenses that are not captured by basic pay, BAH, OHA, BAS, and PCS costs. These costs include overseas station allowances, clothing allowances, Thrift Savings Plan matching, family-separation allowances, separation pay, and the employer's contribution to Social Security. Miscellaneous expenses are estimated by dividing the annual sum of these line items from the service's MILPERS budget by the service's active-duty end strength. FCoM accounts for several costs incurred by DoD that benefit service members but are not directly attributable to specific services. These include discount groceries made available through commissaries on military bases, child development (e.g., day care facilities), programs through the DoD Education Activity that provide for education of service members' children, and programs that provide assistance for military families. Discount groceries are available to current and retired service members, so costs are divided among the retiree and active-duty military populations. Child-development programs, the DoD Education Activity, and family assistance costs are divided by the number of active-duty service members. FCoM also accounts for costs of benefits for service members that accrue to other organizations outside DoD, including Impact Aid, concurrent receipts, and veterans' benefits. Impact Aid is a program by the U.S. Department of Education that provides financial assistance to school districts serving students from military families both on and off base. FCoM accounts for this cost by dividing it across the number of active-duty service members. Concurrent receipt is the simultaneous receipt of two benefits: one from the military retirement benefit and the other from VA disability compensation (Kamarck, 2019). The cost of concurrent receipt is incurred by the Treasury. FCoM accounts for this cost by dividing it by the sum of retirees and active-duty service members. FCoM also accounts for the cost of veterans' benefits provided by the VA by dividing the VA's budget across the veteran population (OSD, CAPE, 2017a).

Finally, direct costs in FCoM reflect the annual costs of recruitment and advertising and training of MILPER, which reflect a service's costs incurred as part of personnel development. These costs are divided evenly across each service's active component end strength. Because the 2019 NDAA isolated G/FO training costs from FCoM as a separate cost category (see Table 2.1), we do not include training costs when estimating G/FO direct costs but retain training costs when reporting direct costs of support personnel.

Direct costs associated with civilians serving in the federal civil service include their direct compensation, overhead costs associated with benefits and insurance, and several other miscellaneous costs (see Table 2.3). Congress sets base pay annually, and it is reflected in the service component's annual O&M budget and accounts for local market supplements. Consequently, base pay is location, grade, and step dependent.[1] FCoM applies a series of overhead cost adjustments. The first adjustment accounts for overtime and holiday pays and incentive and performance awards and depends only on grade and location (OSD, CAPE, 2019). A second overhead cost adjustment is made to reflect fringe benefits (e.g., retirement benefit contributions) and is component dependent in addition to being grade and location dependent. FCoM treats these rates as paid by the services and uses a fringe-benefit factor directed by the OSD comptroller to be used for obtaining reimbursement from other DoD components or federal agencies (McAndrew, 2018). A final overhead cost adjustment accounts for benefit costs paid to former personnel, such as severance payments, and is not service dependent (OSD, CAPE, 2019). These overhead costs reflect rates reported by the OSD comptroller as part of its annual O&M budget requests to Congress and specific guidance on fringe benefits (OSD, CAPE, 2019). Additional costs associated with civilians include training costs, which are included in each service's annual O&M budget request. FCoM estimates this cost by dividing the total training cost by the total number of U.S. direct-hire civilians. Civilians serving overseas are entitled to discounted groceries and an overseas cost of living adjustment. FCoM accounts for the cost of discount groceries by using the same value for military service members. The overseas cost of living adjustment accounts for the price of goods and services compared with Washington, D.C., and is using rates published by the U.S. Department of State. These rates are published multiple times per year, and we base our estimates on the

---

[1]   OPM (undated) states

> Each grade has 10 step rates (steps 1–10) that are each worth approximately 3 percent of the employee's salary. Within-grade step increases are based on an acceptable level of performance and longevity (waiting periods of 1 year at steps 1–3, 2 years at steps 4–6, and 3 years at steps 7–9). It normally takes 18 years to advance from step 1 to step 10 within a single GS [general schedule] grade if an employee remains in that single grade. However, employees with outstanding (or equivalent) performance ratings may be considered for additional, quality step increases (maximum of one per year).

Table 2.3
Civilian Direct Cost Elements

FCoM Manpower Cost Element	FCoM Data Source[a]	Government Organization Bearing Cost	Location Dependent	Grade Dependent	Step Dependent	Service Dependent
Base pay	OPM general and executive pay schedules	Component	X	X	X	
Overtime/holiday pays and incentive/performance awards	OSD comptroller: annual O&M budget requests	Component	X	X	X	
Civilian fringe benefits	OSD comptroller: annual O&M budget requests	Component	X	X	X	X
Severance pay/benefits	OSD comptroller: annual O&M budget requests	Component	X	X	X	
Training	OSD comptroller: annual O&M budget requests	Component				X
Discount groceries-outside continental United States only	OSD comptroller: DoD budget financial summary tables	DoD				
Postretirement life insurance	OPM annual budget documents	Federal government				
Postretirement health benefit	OPM annual budget documents	Federal government				

NOTE: FCoM model cost elements for civilians are defined in OSD, CAPE (2019).
[a] The cost element or the information required to compute the cost element as described in the text can be found on the listed data providers' websites.

rates during the first week in January 2018. FCoM also accounts for contributions to postretirement civil-service benefits that are borne by the federal government and not directly by DoD. These include contributions to the Federal Employee Group Life Insurance and Federal Employee Health Benefit Program. The cost of the benefits per worker are reported in the OPM annual budget request to Congress.

When estimating the direct costs of military positions, we must make assumptions regarding the factors listed in Table 2.2, including rank, location, and years of service. We collected data from the DMDC on personnel and pay for members of the active and reserve components as well as the DoD civilian workforce. Because characteristics of people who fill a position can change over time, we collected data covering FY 2013–2018. For any position for which we estimated direct cost, pay grade reflects the authorized grade for that position at the end of FY 2018. The location used in estimating costs reflects the modal location of personnel in the unit associated with the position in FY 2018. The years of service used in estimating costs reflects the distribution of years of service for personnel holding that pay grade between FY 2013 and FY 2018.[2] By accounting for location in direct costs, our G/FO cost estimates for specific positions will capture greater personnel costs associated with having G/FO positions located in more-expensive civilian housing markets or overseas.

Similarly, when estimating the direct costs of civilian positions, we make assumptions regarding the factors listed in Table 2.3, including grade, location, and step. FCoM is currently designed only to estimate costs for civilians on the federal government's general schedule (GS). For civilians on the Defense Civilian Intelligence Personnel System pay schedule (GG), we assume the equivalent grade on the GS schedule (e.g., a GG-11 is the equivalent of a GS-11), which is consistent with current implementation of this pay schedule (Seacord, 2019). For other pay schedules, we assume individuals receive the pay of a GS-11. As with service members, location used in estimating costs reflects the modal location of personnel (military and civilian) in the unit associated with the position in FY 2018. The step used in estimating costs reflects the distribution of steps for civilian personnel holding that pay grade in the Army between FY 2013 and FY 2018.[3]

G/FO and Staff Travel Costs

We collected data on G/FO and G/FO staff travel costs from DTMO, which oversees the Defense Travel System (DTS). Additionally, we collected data on military air transport (MILAIR) from the Joint Operational Support Airlift Center (JOSAC).

DTS collects travel data for most DoD personnel. As travel is booked by individuals, not by position, accounting for travel costs requires linking positions with personnel. We follow the same approach in identifying travel costs for G/FO and support staff positions. Using monthly DMDC personnel data,[4] we identified all personnel within one grade (+/–1) of a particular position in a unit, as identified by the UIC. We requested travel costs for these individuals from DTMO on all travel for months in unit. To minimize our data request, where possible, we required identified personnel to have the same duty occupation as the authorized position. The travel data collected includes airfare, lodging, per diem, and other miscellaneous costs paid.

---

[2] The distribution of years of service reflects the average of the 10th, 30th, 50th, 70th, and 90th percentiles of all personnel with the same service and pay grade between FY 2013 and FY 2018.

[3] The distribution of steps reflects the average of the 10th, 30th, 50th, 70th, and 90th percentiles of personnel holding that pay grade in the Army between FY 2013 and FY2018. Army civilians are used because their records are the most consistently connected in the DMDC data with the UICs of the service members they are jointly serving with. Civilians in other services appear to frequently be assigned to different unit identification codes (UICs).

[4] We used monthly extracts of DMDC's active duty, reserve, and civilian master and transaction files and the active-duty and reserve pay files from FYs 2013–2018.

Certain G/FOs are entitled to travel on military aircraft as part of their official duties. Department of Defense Directive 4500.56 (2019) establishes four tiers for government air travel. Tier one officials are required to use government aircraft for official and unofficial travel, while tier two travelers are entitled to use government aircraft for official travel. Tier three and four travelers are permitted to use U.S. government aircraft for official travel, but these individuals should defer to using commercial air travel when possible. The CJCS and the vice chairman of the Joint Chiefs of Staff are tier one, while the military service chiefs, combatant commanders, and the commander of U.S. Forces Korea (USFK) are considered tier two travelers. Additionally, the commander of U.S. Forces–Afghanistan (USFOR-A) is considered a tier two traveler while in the United States. We include only government air travel costs for personnel that are required users (tiers one and two), consistent with OSD, CAPE (2017b). We collected all government air travel from JOSAC between FY 2013 and FY 2018 for G/FOs in tiers one and two.

For a G/FO position, we averaged all travel costs observed by G/FOs serving in the same unit as the G/FO position from FY 2013 to FY 2018.[5] Travel records link to specific personnel, not specific positions. Consequently, we average costs when multiple G/FO positions of the same grade exist in a unit (e.g., service chiefs will often be in the same unit). For support personnel, travel costs are only included if they correspond with a G/FO's travel itinerary in their unit. In order for travel to correspond and to identify individuals that went on the same trip, we require the support staff to be in the same UIC as the G/FO (except protection details), to travel to the same destination, have travel dates overlap or begin up to one week prior (to accommodate advance teams), and have the same trip purpose (such as site visit or special mission travel). To identify individuals in protection-providing organizations, we identify trips using the same criteria, except we use UICs associated with protection-providing organizations instead of the same UIC as the G/FO. For G/FOs required to use government aircraft and their support personnel, their travel (including per diem) is still reported in DTS. In these cases, airfare costs will be zero in DTS, but information on government aircraft, including plane type, flight crew size and composition, and flight hours, is reflected in data that JOSAC provided. Based on plane type and flight hours, we use information that JOSAC provided to assign aggregated costs for a given position. That cost for military air travel is incorporated into the G/FO's travel costs.

Using the above procedure, we are able to associate travel records with 88 percent of Army G/FOs, 91 percent of Navy, 72 percent of Marine Corps, 96 percent of Air Force, and 51 percent of joint G/FOs. For the Marine Corps, DMDC's duty unit identifier reflects the resource-utilization code, which does not uniquely identify

---

[5] We developed an annualized cost based on the number of years the G/FO position appeared. For example, if a position existed only from FY 2016 to FY 2018, then it would reflect the average annual travel costs over three years.

units. Additionally, all Marine Corps GOs are affiliated with a common-duty unit in DMDC's personnel records. Therefore, we are unable to directly associate individual travel costs with any Marine Corps GO position. To identify support staff for Marine Corps GOs, we identified an alternative UIC based on the number of people and the number of recorded trips that Marine Corps service members took with the GO. If an individual traveled to the same destination and departed and returned the same week, we categorized this as a potential trip a Marine Corps service member took with the GO. Because non-GO marines generally have a unit identifier that links back to a specific unit, we link Marine Corps GOs with their specific position by using the unit identifier of the personnel that travel with them.

Accounting for travel costs requires linking positions with personnel. DMDC's personnel data, however, cannot currently be linked to specific positions in service and joint organizations. As a result, the personnel for whom we requested travel information from DTMO may be an incomplete record of all support personnel. Consequently, our estimates are likely an underestimate of actual G/FO support travel costs.

G/FO Official Residences

Some MILPER are assigned government quarters. Certain quarters are set aside for specific G/FO positions. In these circumstances, the G/FO does not receive a BAH to offset the management and maintenance costs of those quarters (OSD, CAPE, 2017b). OSD, CAPE (2017b) noted several other rationales for G/FO official residences, including required equipment, such as security systems, antiterrorism measures, and a Sensitive Compartmented Information Facility. The service responsible for an installation manages the official residences on that installation. The costs for service-owned and privately leased quarters are reported annually as part of the "General and Flag Officer Quarters" budget exhibit. Only quarters with annual maintenance costs exceeding a threshold of $35,000 for government-owned and $50,000 for privately leased quarters are reported. As upkeep and maintenance costs may be sporadic, we collected all addresses reported between FY 2009 and FY 2018. We provided these addresses to the applicable service official residence management offices, who then collected information on which G/FOs resided at those locations in each year.[6]

Because G/FO BAH is already accounted for in our FCoM cost estimates, we need only an additional estimate of G/FO quarters costs that exceed BAH. To create the estimate, we created an average annual upkeep and maintenance cost for an official residence based on the reported costs for that address between FY 2009 and FY 2018.[7] In years that the address was not reported, we assigned a zero. We assigned a nonzero

---

[6] These offices are Marine Corps Housing Program; U.S. Air Force Housing, Asset Management Division; Navy Housing Programming & Resource Manager (N93); and Army Housing Division.

[7] Costs are inflated in 2018 dollars using the U.S. Department of Commerce's consumer price index for urban consumers.

cost for quarters if the average annual upkeep and maintenance costs for the official residence exceeded the G/FO's BAH based on his or her rank and location. Because these upkeep and maintenance costs are sporadic, in many cases, a G/FO's BAH exceeded the average annual upkeep and maintenance costs.

The services provided information on positions associated with addresses of the quarters we collected (regardless of rank). The information collected from the services revealed turnover in the positions held by the G/FO occupants, particularly at installations with many G/FO residences. In these cases, we assigned the G/FO position associated with the last G/FO to live in that residence. In cases where the last person to live in multiple houses filled the same G/FO position, we affiliated the most recent residence with the G/FO position.

G/FO Training Costs

Section 596 of the 2019 NDAA required the use of FCoM for estimating training costs. OSD, CAPE (2017a) states that FCoM training costs reflect a service's total training costs divided by its end strength.[8] In Chapters Three and Four, we report the FCoM training costs. FCoM training costs in FY 2018 were $4,737 for the Air Force, $7,853 for the Army, $5,153 for the Marine Corps, and $3,236 for the Navy.

FCoM does not reflect G/FO-specific training costs. There are G/FO-specific training courses sponsored by the National Defense University (NDU) and other service-specific training courses. All new O-7s are required to attend CAPSTONE to increase their effectiveness in planning and employing U.S. forces in joint and combined operations (Chairman of the Joint Chief of Staff Instruction 1801.01D, 2015). O-9s are required to attend PINNACLE to provide these prospective joint and combined force commanders with an understanding of national policy objectives, international implications, and the development of operational campaign plans (Chairman of the Joint Chief of Staff Instruction 1801.01D, 2015). NDU administers both CAPSTONE and PINNACLE. We collected data from NDU on the recent cost per participant in these courses. CAPSTONE is a five-week course that requires substantial travel (typically using government aircraft) and has six personnel dedicated to it. DTS costs were excluded, as these would be captured in other travel costs. PINNACLE is five days, has two staff dedicated to it, and requires no substantial travel. For a CAPSTONE attendee, the average cost of the course was $40,051, and for a PINNACLE attendee, the average cost of the course was $21,902. Because a G/FO receives training over the remainder of his or her career, we amortize these training costs over the average years remaining until retirement for a new one-star G/FO for CAPSTONE (7.8 years) and for a new three-star G/FO for PINNACLE (4.7 years). We find that the average annual cost for these NDU courses are $5,135 for G/FOs in pay grades O-7 and O-8

---

[8] A service's annual training costs are reported in the service comptroller's annual budget request's O&M documentation. The service's end strength is the MILPERS documentation.

(reflecting CAPSTONE only) and $9,795 for G/FOs in pay grades O-9 and O-10 (reflecting CAPSTONE and PINNACLE). These costs exceed the FCoM training costs for most services.

We also collected information from the Army, Navy, and Marine Corps on service-specific G/FO training. Available data differ considerably among these services. For example, not all services are able to provide training estimates disaggregated by G/FO rank. Therefore, we interpreted these data with caution, but we expect that they likely represent the magnitude of G/FO-specific service training costs. Averaging across all service and grade combinations for which we have data, we estimate service-specific training to cost an average of $5,000 per year for each G/FO undertaking training, with the highest average observed for any service grade combination being $8,000 per year.[9]

In addition to courses from NDU and service war colleges, G/FOs may receive additional training from nonmilitary academic institutions. None of our training cost estimates reflect the cost of these courses. However, relative to other G/FO costs, such as the cost of supporting personnel, we expect these costs to be minor. For example, consider a one-time course for an O-7 with a fee of $20,000. Once this fee is annualized over a G/FO's career (e.g., 4.7 years for an O-7), the annual training cost would be approximately $4,255. In comparison, the FCoM estimated annual direct cost of one supporting civilian administrative aide with pay grade GS-11 in Washington, D.C., is $115,000 (this value reflects the cost elements reported in Table 2.3).

Although FCoM training costs do not reflect G/FO-specific training, based on the data we collected from NDU and the services, we find that FCoM training cost estimates and G/FO-specific training cost estimates are of the same order of magnitude (e.g., costs range from $3,000 to $10,000). These costs are an order of magnitude smaller than costs associated with personnel.

G/FO Personal Security Detail Costs

Section 596 of the 2019 NDAA specifically called out the cost of providing security to G/FOs as a required cost category. Certain G/FO positions qualify for personal security details (PSDs) given the nature of their positions. DoDI O-2000.22 establishes the policy for the designation and protection of high-risk personnel (HRP). It designates the size of PSDs and tasks specific agencies with providing those details. It also designates five levels of protection and designates principals (typically civilian DoD leaders and G/FOs) associated with those levels of protection. OSD, CAPE (2017b), from which

---

[9] This training cost should be distributed across the time for which that training was valuable to the G/FO's duties (e.g., the cost of CAPSTONE was distributed across the G/FO's expected remaining time in service). However, we were unable to link courses taken back to G/FOs or establish a panel of trainings received by G/FOs. We expect that G/FOs receive less than one training per year on average, and we expect the value of that training to last for more than one year, so we would expect that the annualized cost of training for a specific G/FO from these war colleges to be less than $5,000.

we paraphrase key details, provides additional detail surrounding the instruction. The level with the most substantial PSD is HRP level 1 enhanced, which provides designated principals with continuous security and authorizes between 25 to 31 personnel for their protective detail. This includes the CJCS and vice chairman of the Joint Chiefs of Staff. HRP level 1 provides designated principals with continuous security and authorizes protections details of 14–20 personnel. HRP level 2 provides designated principals with continuous security during periods of official duty and official travel and authorizes protection details of 6–9 personnel. Principals designated HRP level 2.5 receive protection on foreign travel, and HRP level 3 principals receive additional personal protection–related training. For the purposes of this report, we estimate G/FO PSD costs for G/FOs receiving continuous protection as part of their official duties, which reflect G/FOs designated as HRP levels 1 enhanced, 1, and 2 principals. The U.S. Army Criminal Investigation Command, Naval Criminal Investigative Service, and the Air Force Office of Special Investigations provide protection details. We refer to these organizations collectively as protection-providing organizations (PPOs).

Our cost estimate of security for G/FOs includes three parts: the direct costs of positions reported to be part of G/FO PSDs, any extraordinary equipment required for G/FO PSDs, and travel of G/FO protection detail personnel. We estimated each of these costs and then associated the costs with specific G/FO positions. To estimate these costs and associate them with a specific G/FO position, we collected from each PPO the identifiers of the units responsible for providing PSDs, manpower composition of the PSDs, and equipment costs.

We calculated protection detail direct costs based on reported composition of each G/FO's protection detail collected during conversations with PPOs and a review of relevant unit manning documents. These provided number, ranks, and status (military or civilian) for each authorized position in the protective details. We estimated costs for each authorized position in the detail using FCoM just as we did for other support staff.

Extraordinary equipment required additional data from the PPOs. We collected data on equipment and cost, including both procurement and annual maintenance, for each PPO. PPOs identified a variety of equipment required for protection details, including handheld explosive detectors, light and siren car kits, surveillance kits, wireless communication equipment, handheld radios, earpieces, and commercial and armored cars.

Most of these items last for several years and are replaced as required rather than on fixed schedules. PPOs varied in their ability to identify costs and useful lifespan for these items, which made it difficult to assign annual costs to equipment. Furthermore, equipment was not always consistently purchased for specific protection details. Instead, the equipment was purchased for use by the PPO for all protection details.

Given considerable variance in data reported, we harmonized equipment used across PPOs to produce a per-detail cost estimate of the equipment required to protect a G/FO.[10] We estimate this amount to be $35,000 annually. This does not include the costs of armored cars because of inconsistent availability of data and inconsistent provision of armored cars (e.g., the armored car used by the CJCS is purchased by his office rather than the PPO responsible for his protective detail). The average extraordinary equipment cost for a protection detail and the direct cost of the detail are reported as part of G/FO PSD costs for G/FO positions warranting continuous protection.

We collected travel costs for protection details in a similar manner to other support staff, with some key differences. Each PPO provided the study team with a series of UICs that were used for G/FO PSDs. We associate travel costs of personnel assigned to those UICs with a G/FO's travel if that travel was concurrent with a G/FO receiving continuous protection by a PPO, as with travel costs of other staff. Security detail travel costs are reported as part of staff travel for relevant G/FO positions.

Identifying G/FO Positions

We identified specific G/FO positions based on authorized positions reported in manning documents that we collected from the service and joint staff manpower systems (see Appendix B for more detail). We collected manning documents for any organization with at least one G/FO. Manning documents routinely include authorized G/FO positions that remain unfilled because of limitations on the maximum number of G/FOs. We then used additional data provided by the G/FO management offices to eliminate positions that were not filled as of the end of FY 2018 and added positions that were filled but not authorized on the manning documents.

Within the services, we identified units by the UIC. In the case of the joint staff manpower system, we identified an organization by an activity code and an office within an organization (e.g., immediate office of the commander) by a department identification code (DEPTID). We collected information on offices headed by G/FOs and offices that were located "close" to a G/FO's office in the manning document. We

---

[10] PPOs identified different pieces of equipment. We provided each PPO with an opportunity to clarify whether it used certain pieces of equipment and their associated cost. However, efforts at reconciling differences in costs did not result in a logically consistent representation of equipment costs (e.g., PPOs reported substantially different prices for procurement and maintenance of specific equipment items). Consequently, we opted to produce a per-detail cost estimate. To do so, we created a harmonized equipment list reflecting equipment commonly used by the PPOs. Then, using equipment costs provided by the PPOs, we set a common cost per unit. We produced an equipment cost estimate per detail by applying the common cost per unit to the harmonized equipment list.

collected information on these additional offices to capture potential G/FO support staff.[11]

G/FO positions differ substantially by functional area (e.g., commander, director, general/flag staff), nature of position (e.g., operating forces, service chief staff headquarters), and organization type (e.g., material and logistics, military operations). We categorized G/FO positions along these dimensions using existing positional categorizations developed in an earlier study on G/FO requirements (Harrington et al., 2018). We categorized new positions that were created since that study using a similar approach.

Manning documents typically include more G/FO authorizations than there are available G/FOs to fill those positions. G/FO authorized positions for which a G/FO is not available either go unfilled or are filled by a military officer of lower rank. The number of G/FOs on active duty is limited by law. 10 U.S. Code § 526 establishes maximum limits for active-duty G/FOs by service and for joint duty assignments, and 10 U.S. Code § 525 establishes limits for specific G/FO grades by service and for joint-duty assignments. We restricted our cost-estimation analysis to G/FO positions that are filled by individuals counting toward active-duty statutory limits. Table 2.4 compares our collected sample of positions from service and joint organization manning documents relative to the maximum authorizations. For the services, the maximum number of O-10 positions are filled at the end of FY 2018, while lower ranks are often underfilled. The underfilling of authorized G/FOs may reflect reductions in preparation for the mandated G/FO reduction by December 31, 2022, required in 10 U.S. Code § 526a.

Manning documents occasionally misrepresented authorized G/FO positions. In various circumstances, we were able to verify that a position that was reported as not authorized at the end of FY 2018 was in fact filled. Examples include the chief and vice chief of the National Guard Bureau (these positions count toward active-duty G/FO authorizations), the commander of the U.S. European Command, the commander of U.S. Indo-Pacific Command, the commander of USFK, Commander of USFOR-A. This is not an exhaustive list. For O-10 and O-9 positions, we used data provided by the study sponsor to confirm positions that were filled as of the end of FY 2018.

At the end of the study, we identified approximately 40 G/FO positions for which we had no manning documents. These included positions at the North Atlantic Treaty Organization (NATO) headquarters, Joint Special Operations Command, Office of Military Commissions, the F-35 Joint Strike Fighter program, Joint Artificial Intelligence Center, DoD Sexual Assault Prevention and Response Office, Combined

---

[11] We determined closeness by the DEPTID. DEPTIDs have up to ten characters and are sufficient to identify G/FOs but may not be sufficient to identify G/FO support staff. We considered offices close to a G/FO's office if their DEPTIDs were similar to a G/FO's DEPTID but differed in the last three characters of the DEPTID. For example, if the G/FO DEPTID was B123456000, then we would collect such offices as B123456001 and B123456100 but not offices that differed in the first seven digits.

Table 2.4
G/FO Positions Identified by Service

Grade	Army Max. Auth.	Army Sample	Navy Max. Auth.	Navy Sample	Marines Corps Max. Auth.	Marines Corps Sample	Air Force Max. Auth.	Air Force Sample	Joint Max. Auth.	Joint Sample
O-10	7	7	6	6	2	2	9	9	20	15
O-9	39[a]	34	27[a]	27	15[a]	15	35[a]	28	48[a]	40[b]
O-8	90	82	50	42	22	22	73	49	144	89[c]
O-7	95[c]	101[d]	79[c]	74	23[c]	22	81[c]	94[d]	98[c]	110[b]
Total	231	224	162	149	62	61	198	180	310	254[b]

NOTES: Max. Auth. = maximum authorization; this reflects the total number of active-duty G/FOs authorized for each service and joint duty assignments in 10 U.S. Code § 526, and the maximum authorized active-duty G/FOs in each grade reflects the caps set in 10 U.S. Code § 525. The sample reflects the number of filled G/FO position authorizations that we identified using billets provided to this study. The sample excludes G/FOs that are rotating or positions for which manning documents could not be collected, as discussed in the main text.
[a] 10 U.S. Code § 525 establishes a cap for O-9 and O-10s combined as well as a separate cap for O-10s, so the amounts represented in the table indicate the residual number of authorizations for O-9 conditional on all O-10 authorizations being filled.
[b] The joint duty positions are an undercount of G/FOs serving in joint duty assignments as of the end of FY 2018. See text for details.
[c] O-7 authorizations are not specifically set out in 10 U.S. Code § 525, so the values reported reflect the difference between the total number of G/FO authorizations in 10 U.S. Code § 526 and the number in grades O-8 to O-10 assuming each grade is filled with its maximum authorized positions.
[d] The Army and Air Force sample of O-7s exceeds the reported maximum authorization because the total of higher pay grades is below the maximum authorized level for those grades, allowing additional space for O-7 GOs.

Joint Task Force–Operation Inherence Resolve, 509th Bomber Wing, Army Intelligence and Security Command, Naval Region Mariana, and various headquarters positions in the services. Additionally, there were various G/FO positions that were in transition in September 2018. If an O-9 or O-10 position was in transition but normally filled, it was included in the cost estimates.

DMDC (September 2018) reports that there were 921 active duty G/FOs at the end of FY 2018, which is close to the 919 positions either reported in Table 2.4 or identified as missing from the manning documents provided for this study.[12] G/FO positions are routinely in flux. At times, it is possible for an O-6 (non-G/FO) position to be temporarily filled by a G/FO, and temporary G/FO positions are sometimes created to address current issues requiring senior military leadership. Recognizing

---

[12] We identified seven missing G/FO positions that were filled for the Air Force; three missing G/FO positions that were filled for the Army; six missing G/FO positions for the Navy; one missing G/FO position for the Marine Corps; and 34 missing G/FO positions that were filled in joint duty assignments.

these limitations, we conclude that our sample largely represents the population of G/FO positions filled at the end of FY 2018.

Categorizing G/FO Support Positions

OSD, CAPE (2017b) identified two broad G/FO support categories: personal and positional support. Personal support are staff under the G/FO's immediate control that support the G/FO personally, including aides-de-camp, enlisted aides, drivers, and security details (if assigned). Positional support are staff who support the G/FO's mission and are not charged with managing the G/FO's personal matters. These include executive and administrative assistants, executive officers, and other positions whose work supports the G/FO's mission. Staff in roles that support the organization (e.g., a commanding general's deputy) are considered organizational support staff and are not included in the cost estimates.

Consistent with this definition of positional support, and with concurrence from our sponsor, we included staff serving in protocol positions and in commander's action groups (CAGs) (also known as commander initiative groups and strategic initiative groups) as G/FOs' positional support. Protocol staff are responsible for planning and executing representational events and official functions (such as arranging visits for dignitaries, official entertaining, and military ceremonies). CAG staff are assigned tasks in support of their senior leader's mission and organizational responsibilities, including speechwriting and preparation of other types of communication, such as congressional testimony; undertaking special projects, such as strategic reviews; advising commanders on specialized topics; and meeting functions, such as note-taking, summarizing results, and assigning tasks to offices across the organization. OSD, CAPE (2017b) also stated that chaplains, inspectors general, public affairs officers, and staff judge advocates were positional staff. We believe, and the research sponsor concurred, that these positions are inconsistent with the definition of positional support staff because they support the organization's mission, not the G/FO's mission. We exclude these staff in our cost estimates.

Manning documents do not consistently identify G/FO support, and OSD, CAPE (2017b) did not establish a categorization method. To ensure a consistent categorization, we developed a categorization of support personnel into eight categories:

- personal support (i.e., support a G/FO's personal matters)
  - aides-de-camp
  - enlisted aides
  - other personal support (e.g., drivers)

- positional support (i.e., support a G/FO's mission)
  - executive officers
  - civilian administrative assistants
  - enlisted executive assistants
  - protocol staff
  - CAG staff.

As noted in the previous section, we collected all authorized positions in manning documents with at least one authorized G/FO position. Based on position description and grade, we applied a common set of textual rules to categorize support staff based on having the same UIC/DEPTID. For example, if a title included "XO", we categorized it as an executive officer. We made special exceptions after review of each service's billets (e.g., in the Navy, if the title included "FLAG SEC" and it was an officer, then it was categorized as an executive officer). Service-specific documentation for each support position's categorization is available in Appendix B.

Associating G/FO Support Positions with Specific G/FO Positions

All authorized G/FO support positions associated with a G/FO are included in staff direct cost estimates for that G/FO. However, not all staff categorized as personal and positional staff are associated with a G/FO (rather, they are associated with more-junior officers or other offices within that unit). We identify authorized positions likely associated with providing personal or positional support to a G/FO in a UIC (services) or DEPTID (joint duty assignments) by

- identifying the highest rank within a UIC or DEPTID
- identifying positions assigned to a unique UIC/DEPTID whose highest pay grade is a G/FO that would be treated as positional or personal staff if they share the same DEPTID or UIC–office identifier (OFFICEID) combination as the G/FO.[13]

For DEPTIDs or UIC-OFFICEID with multiple G/FOs, we assign support staff to the highest-ranking G/FO first, then second, and so on. If the number of support staff exceed the number of G/FOs, excess support staff are then assigned first to the highest G/FO, then to the second highest, and so on. There is an exception where

---

[13] We developed office identifiers (i.e., delineations of offices within a unit) based on service manning documents. By service, we used the office symbol code in the Air Force; paragraph number in the Army; and the first two characters of the billet sequence code in the Navy. For the Marine Corps, office delineations are reported as separate records on the manning document, so we created our own office identifier based on where the office records were reported on the manning documents relative to positional billets.

protocol and CAGs are associated with the highest-ranking G/FO in a DEPTID or UIC-OFFICEID.

Although the majority of G/FO support staff had the same UIC-OFFICEID or DEPTID as the G/FO they supported, we identified several deviations. For O-10 and O-9 joint staff assignments, the Marine Corps, and a few of the other services' units, we manually recategorized positions that were assigned to a different DEPTID or UIC-OFFICEID if we could identify that they should be assigned to a G/FO. This most often came up when administrative, protocol, and CAG staff were assigned to a separate office rather than the G/FO's immediate office. This also arose in the Air Force, where the Chief of Staff of the Air Force (CSAF) is the only service member assigned his or her UIC. In this case, the CSAF's support staff is associated with the Air Staff. In these cases, we assigned everyone to the same DEPTID or UIC-OFFICEID prior to applying the G/FO association process above.

We implemented a special process for associating enlisted aides with G/FOs. Enlisted aides are often not included on the G/FO's manning documents, are managed separately, and are subject to overall caps. OSD's Senior Officer Matters office regularly collects information on enlisted aides that includes their assigned G/FO's position. Using this information, we drop any enlisted aides reported on manning documents and import the counts from this independent list. Reflecting that they are managed centrally by the services, we assume enlisted aides are ranked E-6 with ten years of service for the purposes of costing.

See Appendix B for service-specific documentation for the association of support personnel.

Framework Overview and Limitations

In this chapter, we described our framework for estimating G/FO and G/FO support costs that includes definitions of cost elements; a method for estimating the cost of each element; and an approach for identifying specific G/FO and G/FO support positions, categorizing G/FO support positions, and associating G/FO support with specific G/FO positions. Once a G/FO position is identified as filled, then potential authorized support positions are identified, categorized, and associated with that G/FO. Then, we apply the direct costing methods to the G/FO and G/FO support positions (including protection details where required) described in this chapter conditional on

- authorized grade in manning documents
- distribution of years of service in that service (military) or distribution of steps in the Army (civilian) for personnel in that pay grade based on DMDC's military and civilian personnel files from FY 2013 to FY 2018

- modal location of service members at the end of FY 2018 in the G/FO's unit estimated from DMDC's MILPER and pay files.

These direct costs are estimated using our adaptation of OSD CAPE's FCoM model. OSD CAPE set up the FCoM model to estimate the cost of one position at a time. As this study required estimating thousands of G/FO and G/FO support positions, we extended FCoM to estimate staff costs in bulk. We tested the output of our adapted FCoM model against OSD CAPE's FCoM model to ensure that we estimated similar numbers.

We added other costs to the direct costs. These other costs include G/FO protection detail costs, G/FO and support staff travel costs, the cost of G/FO official residences in excess of BAH, and G/FO training costs.

In this chapter, we identified three fundamental limitations in costing specific G/FO positions and their support personnel. First, the data we had access to did not enable us to directly link a person to an authorized position. This affects the association of travel costs (which are person-specific) to a G/FO position. This limitation is most likely to affect G/FO positions for which there are multiple G/FOs of the same rank in the same unit (e.g., headquarters staff).

Second, existing manpower data systems for manning documents that track authorized positions vary across the services and joint duty assignments, and categorizations tend not to be consistent within these organizations. This affects the ability to consistently categorize support staff and associate them to a specific G/FO position. This limitation is most likely to affect organizations that associate many G/FO positions with a common unit (e.g., Marine Corps and Navy) or organizations that have inconsistent coding of position terminology.

Finally, existing data systems are subject to user input error. We observed this in several circumstances, most notably when some O-10 combatant commanders and all USFOR-A positions were recorded as not authorized at the end of FY 2018. This affects the ability to identify authorized positions and associate person-level information to a specific G/FO position. This limitation is most likely to affect organizations whose positional information requires frequent updating (e.g., joint positions require frequent updating to reflect person-specific information such as service and service UIC).

We documented our efforts in this chapter and Appendix B to correct for these limitations, but these corrections are unlikely to fully resolve them. These limitations have consequences for the interpretation and use of the G/FO cost estimates presented in this report. We recommend that users of these cost estimates be cautious when making comparisons across services or with joint positions. Differences in costs could reflect inconsistency in reporting positions by organization. These inconsistencies may have resulted in miscategorization that has the potential to bias cost estimates if too many or too few staff positions are affiliated with a G/FO position. Additionally, cost differences may reflect unobserved differences in operations. Officials from senior officer management offices told us that some G/FOs receive support from personnel who are assigned another task. We cannot identify informal G/FO support by our approach.

Context (i.e., differences in positional characteristics and data quality by service) affects differences in position-specific costs and may affect applicable comparisons. For example, travel costs will be greater for G/FOs required to use government aircraft. Given the nature of this requirement, the applicable comparison may be a charter flight rather than commercial coach fares. This important context is noted when reporting G/FO cost estimates.

The G/FO cost estimates provided in this report are total costs of G/FO positions and reflect characteristics of the G/FO position and varying quality of data that are used to estimate costs. If this cost-estimating framework is repeated, then total costs can be used to identify trends in overall G/FO costs as well as specific underlying G/FO cost elements. G/FO positions vary in several key characteristics, including location, nature of position, organizational type, and function. G/FO positions by service may also vary along these positional characteristics. As discussed in the first chapter, the appropriate G/FO cost measure to use in an analysis or to report in a publication depends on the purpose for using or reporting a G/FO cost estimate. Most often, cost estimates are used for comparative purposes (e.g., changing authorized rank of a G/FO position), in which case a marginal cost measure is most appropriate.

The cost estimates reported in the next chapters can be used to assess trends in G/FO costs if the cost estimation is repeated over time. However, the cost estimates should not solely be used to justify G/FO positional changes because they do not account for the benefit of having a G/FO position nor do they account for the additional implications of changing a G/FO position as discussed in Chapter One.

CHAPTER THREE

Typical General and Flag Officer Cost Estimates

This chapter describes the average annual cost estimates of a typical G/FO by grade and by service as described in OSD, CAPE (2017b) and required by section 596 of the 2019 NDAA (Pub. L. 115-232, 2018). We first describe the costs included in each estimate, provide the distribution of support staff and average total costs for all G/FOs, and then separately by service. The chapter ends with a discussion of these costs and the limitations of these estimates.

Costs Included in Typical G/FO Estimates

Estimates of a typical G/FO's cost include three sources: direct G/FO costs, G/FO direct staff costs, and G/FO training costs (see Table 2.1 and Chapter Two for additional detail). G/FO and G/FO support direct costs come from our adaptation of CAPE's FCoM model as discussed in Chapter Two.

We derive training costs included in these cost estimates from FCoM. These costs reflect a service's annual cost of training averaged across its active-duty end strength. As a result, these costs do not reflect G/FO-specific training and do not vary by grade or years of service.

Consistent with the recommendations of OSD, CAPE (2017b), some of the costs discussed in Chapter Two are excluded from typical G/FO cost estimates, such as G/FO travel costs, G/FO support staff travel costs, G/FO official residence costs, and G/FO protection detail costs. The excluded costs reflect costs that are position specific and may exhibit greater annual volatility than the cost elements included in estimates of a typical G/FO's cost.

Overall Costs of a Typical G/FO

Table 3.1 presents the average number of support staff by personal and positional support categories by G/FO grade across all services and joint duty assignments. Average support staff increase substantially for senior officer ranks. Personal support

Table 3.1
Typical G/FO Average Support by Grade, All Services

Grade	Aide-de-Camp	Enlisted Aide	Other Personal	Executive Officer	Civilian Administrative Assistant	Enlisted Executive Assistant	Protocol	CAG	Overall
O-7	0.2	0.1	0.1	0.4	0.5	0.4	0.2	0.2	2.1
O-8	0.4	0.1	0.2	0.5	0.6	0.5	0.4	0.4	3.1
O-9	0.4	0.6	0.2	1.1	0.7	0.6	0.7	0.7	5.0
O-10	0.9	2.1	0.4	1.8	0.6	1.9	3.9	3.0	14.7

NOTES: Estimated values use manning documents provided for this study reflecting end of FY 2018. Sample sizes are reported in Table 2.4. This table reflects averages across all services based on these manning documents and applying a common support staff categorization with adjustments for consistency because of differences in service or joint organizations' manning document terminology and structure.

in the form of aides-de-camp and enlisted aides are rare for G/FOs below the rank of O-9. Positional support is larger than personal support at every rank, so it will be the major cost driver in support personnel costs.

Table 3.2 presents the average annual total cost estimates for a typical G/FO by grade. These costs are averaged across all G/FO positions in our sample, in effect weighting each grade by the number of G/FOs of that grade across the services. The cost estimates demonstrate that costs increase with grade and are substantially higher for O-10s than for O-9s (more than double). The increase in costs by grade are primarily associated with positional support staff.

Table 3.2
Average Annual Total Costs (in Thousands) for a Typical G/FO

Grade	G/FO Direct Costs	Staff Direct Costs Personal	Staff Direct Costs Positional	G/FO Training (FCoM)	Total
O-7	$286	$64	$242	$5	$598
O-8	$321	$111	$362	$6	$799
O-9	$336	$198	$645	$5	$1,184
O-10	$336	$559	$2,071	$5	$2,971

NOTES: All costs expressed in 2018 dollars. Costs estimated using FCoM based on assumptions stated in Chapter Two. Training is derived from the FCoM estimate and is not G/FO specific. Uses Washington, D.C., as the location when duty location could not be determined. Sample sizes are reported in Table 2.4.

Costs of a Typical G/FO by Service

Typical Air Force GOs

Table 3.3 presents the average number of personal and positional staff for Air Force GOs by grade. Relative to the overall average reported in Table 3.1, Air Force GOs receive greater than average overall support, but the type of support varies. Air Force GOs tend to receive less personal support and more positional support. For example, protocol and CAG staff are consistently authorized more than the overall average for Air Force GOs above O-7s. This may reflect that these support positions are the most consistently categorized in the Air Force.

Table 3.4 presents our average annual total cost estimates of typical Air Force GOs by grade. Relative to the average total cost of a G/FO across services in Table 3.2, Air Force GOs are estimated to have greater cost at every grade. Costs of personal and positional support staff reflect the overall patterns of use. Less use of personal staff

Table 3.3
Average Number of Support Staff of Typical GO by Grade, Air Force

Grade	Aide-de-Camp	Enlisted Aide	Other Personal	Executive Officer	Civilian Administrative Assistant	Enlisted Executive Assistant	Protocol	CAG	Overall
O-7	0.0	0.1	0.0	0.4	0.9	0.7	0.4	0.1	2.7
O-8	0.1	0.3	0.0	0.8	0.9	0.5	1.0	0.8	4.5
O-9	0.3	0.6	0.0	1.1	1.1	0.6	0.9	1.9	6.4
O-10	1.0	1.8	0.0	1.3	0.8	0.8	4.9	4.2	14.8

NOTES: Estimated values use manning documents reflecting the end of FY 2018. Sample sizes are reported in Table 2.4. This table reflects averages based on Air Force manning documents and applying a common support staff categorization with adjustments for consistency because of differences in service or joint organizations' manning document terminology and structure.

Table 3.4
Average Annual Total Costs (in Thousands) for a Typical GO, Air Force

Grade	G/FO Direct Costs	Staff Direct Costs Personal	Staff Direct Costs Positional	G/FO Training (FCoM)	Total
O-7	$282	$20	$335	$5	$642
O-8	$321	$67	$589	$5	$982
O-9	$333	$140	$904	$5	$1,382
O-10	$332	$460	$2,071	$5	$2,867

NOTES: All costs expressed in 2018 dollars. Costs estimated using FCoM based on assumptions stated in Chapter Two. Training is derived from the FCoM estimate and is not G/FO specific. Uses Washington, D.C., as location for G/FOs when duty location could not be determined. Sample sizes are reported in Table 2.4.

leads to lower personal staff direct costs, while greater use of positional staff leads to greater positional staff direct costs.

Typical Army GOs

Table 3.5 presents the average number of personal and positional staff for Army GOs by grade. Relative to the overall average reported in Table 3.1, Army GOs receive greater than average total support for O-8s, less than average support for O-10s, and roughly average support at the other grades. There are differences in the type of support. Army GOs tend to receive less support from enlisted executive assistants. Army GOs at grades O-7 to O-9 receive greater support than average from personal support and protocol staff.

Table 3.6 presents our average annual total cost estimates of typical Army GOs by grade. Army personnel cost more because of some of the service-specific costs in Table 2.2, leading to higher G/FO direct costs than average at every G/FO grade. Despite greater direct costs per position, overall costs primarily reflect the pattern of

Table 3.5
Average Number of Support Staff of Typical GO by Grade, Army

Grade	Aide-de-Camp	Enlisted Aide	Other Personal	Executive Officer	Civilian Administrative Assistant	Enlisted Executive Assistant	Protocol	CAG	Overall
O-7	0.4	0.1	0.3	0.3	0.4	0.1	0.3	0.2	2.1
O-8	0.7	0.2	0.4	0.4	0.7	0.2	0.6	0.4	3.5
O-9	0.5	0.8	0.3	1.4	0.6	0.3	0.9	0.3	5.1
O-10	0.7	1.6	0.6	1.7	0.7	1.7	1.9	2.6	11.4

NOTES: Estimated values use manning documents reflecting the end of FY 2018. Sample sizes are reported in Table 2.4. This table reflects averages based on Army manning documents and applying a common support staff categorization with adjustments for consistency because of differences in service or joint organizations' manning document terminology and structure.

Table 3.6
Average Annual Total Costs (in Thousands) for a Typical GO, Army

Grade	G/FO Direct Costs	Staff Direct Costs Personal	Staff Direct Costs Positional	G/FO Training (FCoM)	Total
O-7	$289	$114	$181	$8	$592
O-8	$322	$203	$308	$8	$841
O-9	$342	$256	$624	$8	$1,230
O-10	$342	$483	$1,624	$8	$2,457

NOTES: All costs expressed in 2018 dollars. Costs estimated using FCoM based on assumptions stated in Chapter Two. Training is derived from the FCoM estimate and is not G/FO specific. Uses Washington, D.C., as location for G/FOs when duty location could not be determined. Sample sizes are reported in Table 2.4.

staff use, with costs being slightly above average for O-8s and below average for O-10s, while the rest are very close to the average costs displayed in Table 3.2.

Typical Marine Corps GOs

Table 3.7 presents the average number of personal and positional staff for Marine Corps GOs by grade. Relative to the overall average reported in Table 3.1, Marine Corps GOs receive substantially greater average total support at all grades. Unlike the other services, use of different types of support does not consistently increase with higher grades. The greater use of support staff and variability in the type of support staff may reflect differences in the location, function, organization type, or mission of the Marine Corps GOs relative to other services. This highlights the importance of accounting for differences in these characteristics when comparing across services. For example, the only Marine Corps O-10s are the commandant and assistant commandant of the Marine Corps. Therefore, it is more accurate to compare the commandant to other service chiefs rather than O-10s more broadly (these estimates will be presented in the next chapter on specific G/FO costs). Marine Corps GOs at lower grades make greater use of aides-de-camp, other personal support (such as drivers), and enlisted executive assistants compared with the averages presented in Table 3.1.

Table 3.8 presents our average annual total cost estimates of typical Marine Corps GOs by grade. Marine Corps personnel have lower direct costs because of some of the service-specific costs in Table 2.2 (e.g., the direct cost of a Marine Corps O-7 is the lowest among the services). However, lower direct GO costs are generally offset by the greater use of support personnel, resulting in greater overall costs than all the other services for all grades except O-8s. These cost differences likely reflect differences in characteristics of G/FO positions. Marine Corps O-7s are notably more expensive than the average O-7, reflecting greater average support staff. The higher cost, in part, reflects the Marines Corps use of O-7s. The Marine Corps more often uses O-7s in commander positions (compared with headquarters staff): 59 percent compared with

Table 3.7
Average Number of Support Staff of Typical GO by Grade, Marine Corps

Grade	Aide-de-Camp	Enlisted Aide	Other Personal	Executive Officer	Civilian Administrative Assistant	Enlisted Executive Assistant	Protocol	CAG	Overall
O-7	0.5	0.2	0.5	0.2	0.8	1.3	0.6	0.0	4.1
O-8	0.7	0.0	0.7	0.2	0.4	1.2	0.1	0.0	3.4
O-9	0.8	0.7	0.8	0.9	0.7	1.8	1.0	0.0	6.7
O-10	1.5	2.5	0.5	2.0	0.5	3.5	4.0	5.0	19.5

NOTES: Estimated values use manning documents reflecting the end of FY 2018. Sample sizes are reported in Table 2.4. This table reflects averages based on Marine Corps manning documents and applying a common support staff categorization with adjustments for consistency because of differences in service or joint organizations' manning document terminology and structure.

Table 3.8
Average Annual Total Costs (in Thousands) for a Typical GO, Marine Corps

Grade	G/FO Direct Costs	Staff Direct Costs Personal	Staff Direct Costs Positional	G/FO Training (FCoM)	Total
O-7	$283	$184	$361	$5	$833
O-8	$309	$224	$229	$5	$767
O-9	$327	$355	$696	$5	$1,383
O-10	$337	$752	$2,902	$5	$3,996

NOTES: All costs expressed in 2018 dollars. Costs estimated using FCoM based on assumptions stated in Chapter Two. Training is derived from the FCoM estimate and is not G/FO specific. Uses Washington, D.C., as location for G/FOs when duty location could not be determined. Sample sizes are reported in Table 2.4.

24 percent for the Air Force, 43 percent for the Army, and 58 percent for the Navy. Cost of Marine Corps O-9s are commensurate with the costs of Air Force O-9s but greater than O-9s serving in the Army or joint duty assignments.

Typical Navy Flag Officers

Table 3.9 presents the average number of personal and positional staff for Navy GOs by grade. Navy manning documents collected for this study did not include civilian support, so we estimated average civilian support for these positions based on the average from the other services. Relative to the overall average reported in Table 3.1, Navy FOs receive greater than average total support at all grades. Important differences exist in the type of support. Navy FOs tend to receive more support from officer aides, including aides-de-camp and executive officers. Enlisted aides and enlisted executive assistants are

Table 3.9
Typical FO Average Support by Grade, Navy

Grade	Aide-de-Camp	Enlisted Aide	Other Personal	Executive Officer[a]	Civilian Administrative Assistant[a]	Enlisted Executive Assistant	Protocol[a]	CAG[a]	Overall[a]
O-7	0.4	0.1	0.0	0.7	0.5	0.2	0.3	0.5	2.8
O-8	0.3	0.2	0.0	1.0	0.6	0.6	0.5	0.9	4.2
O-9	0.6	0.6	0.1	1.8	0.8	1.1	0.8	1.2	6.9
O-10	1.2	2.7	0.0	2.3	0.7	3.0	2.7	2.9	15.4

NOTES: Estimated values use manning documents reflecting the end of FY 2018. Sample sizes are reported in Table 2.4. This table reflects averages based on Navy manning documents and applying a common support staff categorization with adjustments for consistency because of differences in service or joint organizations' manning document terminology and structure.
[a] Navy manning documents collected for this study did not include civilian support, so we estimated the average number of civilian support staff for these positions based on the averages from the other services. The overall count is updated to reflect this imputation.

also more heavily used by O-10s than average. Authorizations for other personal staff (e.g., drivers) are notably more limited for Navy FOs.

Table 3.10 presents our average annual total cost estimates of typical Navy FOs by grade. Greater authorization of staff at all grades is reflected in greater staff costs across all grades for the Navy.

Typical Joint Duty Assignment G/FOs

Table 3.11 presents the average number of personal and positional staff for joint duty assignment G/FOs by grade. Support staff at some joint duty assignments—particularly those in organizations outside DoD, such as those in the Executive Office of the

Table 3.10
Average Annual Total Costs (in Thousands) for a Typical FO, Navy

Grade	G/FO Direct Costs	Staff Direct Costs Personal	Staff Direct Costs Positional	G/FO Training (FCoM)	Total[a]
O-7	$285	$92	$340	$3	$720
O-8	$320	$90	$572	$3	$985
O-9	$333	$233	$931	$3	$1,500
O-10	$335	$642	$2,009	$3	$2,990

NOTES: All costs expressed in 2018 dollars. Costs estimated using FCoM based on assumptions stated in Chapter Two. Training is derived from the FCoM estimate and is not G/FO specific. Uses Washington, D.C., as location for G/FOs when duty location could not be determined.
[a] Navy manning documents collected for this study did not include civilian support, so average civilian support costs were imputed for these positions based on the averages from the other services. The overall total cost is updated to reflect this imputation. Sample sizes are reported in Table 2.4.

Table 3.11
Typical G/FO Average Support by Grade, Joint Duty Assignments

Grade	Aide-de-Camp	Enlisted Aide	Other Personal	Executive Officer	Civilian Administrative Assistant	Enlisted Executive Assistant	Protocol	CAG	Overall
O-7	0.0	0.0	0.0	0.3	0.3	0.2	0.0	0.1	0.9[a]
O-8	0.1	0.0	0.1	0.4	0.4	0.4	0.0	0.1	1.5[a]
O-9	0.2	0.4	0.0	0.6	0.4	0.2	0.2	0.1	2.1[a]
O-10	0.9	2.1	0.7	1.9	0.5	2.1	4.8	2.3	15.3[a]

NOTES: Estimated values use manning documents reflecting the end of FY 2018. Sample sizes are reported in Table 2.4. Joint positions that are shared with other organizations that manage their personnel independently may not have their staff accurately represented in the table (see text for additional details) as these staffs may not be managed using the manning documents we received for this study. This table reflects averages based on joint manning documents and applying a common support staff categorization with adjustments for consistency because of differences in service or joint organizations' manning document terminology and structure.
[a] Because of incomplete support staff reflected in the joint manning documents, these levels of average support are likely an underestimate of true G/FO support.

President, U.S. Department of Energy, Central Intelligence Agency, National Geospatial Intelligence Agency, and other intelligence agencies—may not be fully reflected on the joint manning documents that DMDC provided because non-DoD organizations manage these positions. Additionally, as noted in Chapter Two, the G/FO counts for O-7 to O-9 are an undercount because the study did not receive manning documents for 34 NATO, Joint Special Operations Command, and other miscellaneous OSD G/FO positions that were filled at the end of FY 2018.

Relative to the overall average reported in Table 3.1, G/FOs in joint duty assignments receive lower-than-average total support for grades O-7 to O-9 and above- average support for O-10s. This pattern in G/FO support likely reflects the nature of the positions filled. For example, 12 of the 15 joint duty assignment O-10s are commanders of combatant commands or major sub–combatant commands (i.e., USFOR-A, USFK), which are likely to require substantial support given the nature of their mission. Alternatively, only four of the 40 O-9s are commanders, with some O-9s serving in capacities where we do not observe their support staff (e.g., associate director of Central Intelligence for Military Affairs; United States Security Coordinator, Israel-Palestinian Authority) or support staff are shared with the person the G/FO supports (e.g., senior military assistant to the Secretary of Defense; military deputy to the Under Secretary of Defense for Personnel and Readiness). Given the nature of these positions, joint duty–assigned G/FOs below the O-10 grade rarely have personal support or protocol or CAG staff. O-10 G/FOs in joint positions exhibit average support in most personal and positional support categories for their grade, with the exception of a higher number of protocol support positions.

Table 3.12 presents our average annual total cost estimates of typical G/FOs in joint duty assignments by grade. Lower authorizations of staff at grades O-7 to O-9 lead to substantially lower costs at these grades. As expected from the larger-than-average support staff numbers associated with O-10 joint duty positions, their typical costs are among the highest we estimate.

Summary and Limitations

We find that support staff and average annual total costs of typical G/FO positions increase with G/FO pay grade. The increase in costs, as noted in Table 3.2, is primarily driven by positional support staff (i.e., those staff that support the G/FO's mission).

We find that differences exist across the services and joint duty assignments in the use of support staff. When costs are greater than average, the reason is typically the use of more support staff or greater use of military officers relative to enlisted or civilian support. Differences in support staff and costs may reflect differences in the G/FO positions authorized by the services and for joint duty assignments. For example, although joint duty–assigned O-9 G/FOs are, on average, the least expensive O-9

Table 3.12
Average Annual Total Costs (in Thousands) for a Typical G/FO, Joint Duty Assignments

Grade	G/FO Direct Costs	Staff Direct Costs Personal[a]	Staff Direct Costs Positional[a]	G/FO Training (FCoM)	Total[a]
O-7	$290	$14	$129	$5	$438
O-8	$322	$33	$220	$5	$580
O-9	$338	$106	$269	$5	$719
O-10	$336	$594	$2,194	$5	$3,128

NOTES: All costs expressed in 2018 dollars. Costs estimated using FCoM based on assumptions stated in Chapter Two. Support staff estimated using manning documents provided for this study that reflect end of FY 2018. Joint positions that are shared with other organizations that manage their personnel independently may not have their staff accurately represented in the table (see text for additional details) as these staffs may not be managed using the manning documents we received for this study. Training is derived from the FCoM estimate and is not G/FO specific. Uses Washington, D.C., as location for G/FOs when duty location could not be determined.
[a] Because of incomplete support staff reflected in the joint manning documents, these cost estimates are likely an underestimate of true G/FO support costs. Sample sizes are reported in Table 2.4.

G/FOs across services, they are less likely to be in the position of commander than O-9s in the services and hence may have less need for support staff.

We note several limitations when comparing or using these cost estimates. First, there are important differences in the manning documents provided by the services that may lead to a biased count in the number of support staff, which will then lead to biased cost estimates. To minimize this bias, we applied a common categorization of support staff based on the manning documents provided (see Appendix B).

Second, we are missing various positions, particularly in the O-7 to O-9 grades for joint duty assignments. Third, for some joint duty assignments, particularly those shared with non-DoD organizations that manage their personnel independently of DoD, we do not observe support personnel. This leads to an underestimate of support staff for joint duty assignments as well as the average total costs associated with typical joint duty assignments.

Finally, the FCoM training costs reported in this chapter only reflect servicewide averages for training costs and range from $3,000 to $8,000 per year. As detailed in Chapter Two, we collected cost data from NDU on G/FO-specific training, which we estimated to be $5,135 for O-7 and O-8s and $9,795 for O-9 and O-10s. The Army, Navy, and Marine Corps provided additional information on service-specific training, with these costs averaging $5,000 and not exceeding $8,000. The reported FCoM values generally underestimate the cost of G/FO-specific training, although the underestimate is small relative to direct costs associated with G/FOs and their support staff.

CHAPTER FOUR

Specific G/FO Cost Estimates

This chapter describes our annual total cost estimates of G/FO positions by grade, service, and position characteristics. We calculate costs for all G/FO positions and summarize them in this chapter by key details of the position. Drawing on prior research into G/FO positions (Harrington et al., 2018), we present costs for each grade and service combination by position category,[1] organization type,[2] and functional area.[3] We first describe the costs included in each estimate, and then provide and discuss four examples of specific G/FO cost estimates: (1) a select set of specific O-10 G/FO positions, (2) service and grade G/FO cost estimates by position category, (3) service and grade G/FO cost estimates by organization type, and (4) service and grade G/FO cost estimates by functional area. The chapter ends with a discussion of these costs and the limitations of these estimates. Appendix A provides additional annual total cost estimates for all G/FO positions that required PSDs or government air travel as well as average annual total cost estimates for each service and grade by position category, organization type, and functional area.

Costs Included in Specific G/FO Estimates

Position-specific G/FO cost estimates include all the costs from the typical estimates (see Chapter Three), plus several additional direct and indirect costs. Additional direct

---

[1] Nature of position includes commander, director, Program Executive Officer (PEO)/deputy PEO, deputy or vice commander, chief of staff, deputy director, and general/flag staff.

[2] Organization type includes combatant command; defense joint or service agency; direct reporting unit/share-based bureaus/acquisition activity/supporting establishment/field operating agencies, joint staff, major commands/service commands/type commands; national; operating forces; OSD service chief of staff headquarters; service component commands; and theater.

[3] Function includes acquisition/research and development; command, control, communications, computers, and intelligence (C4I); capabilities development/integration; engineer; force management development education and training, intelligence; manpower and personnel; materiel and logistics; military operations; program management/financial management; special staff; and strategic plans and policy.

costs include personal money allowances as applicable by G/FO position and direct costs of security details for the subset of G/FO positions receiving continuous security protection. These estimates also include a variety of indirect costs in three primary categories: travel, PPO equipment costs, and costs associated with the upkeep and maintenance of G/FO quarters. We account for travel costs, as described in Chapter Two. These costs include both G/FO and staff travel, which includes security details from PPOs. Travel costs include commercial airfare; lodging and per diem; and, for select G/FO positions, MILAIR costs. We also account for the cost of upkeep and maintenance of G/FO quarters above the cost of BAH, as described in Chapter Two.

Cost of G/FO Requiring Daily Protection or Government Air Travel

Table 4.1 presents the support staff for select G/FOs—CJCS and the service chiefs—requiring daily protection. Personal support is similar across these positions, but positional support staff varies. Variation in the assignment of staff to particular categories may reflect terminology in the unit's manning document that leads to a greater number of a particular category of staff (e.g., the Chief of Naval Operations has more enlisted executive assistants, which may partially account for his relatively limited protocol staff). The Air Force Chief of Staff shares a larger CAG with the Secretary of the Air Force. According to our support staff association methodology described in Chapter Two, the CAG staff are associated with the Secretary of the Air Force as the senior official in the unit. A complete list of support staff for G/FOs requiring continuous PSDs or government air travel can be found in Table A.1 in Appendix A.

Table 4.2 presents the position-specific costs for the individual positions requiring daily protective details. These positions are also authorized to use military aircraft for their travel. The use of MILAIR, plus the high rank and greater numbers of positional staff associated with the duties of these G/FOs, lead to substantial costs above a typical O-10 G/FO. A complete list of annual cost estimates for G/FOs requiring continuous PSDs or government air travel is available in Table A.2 in Appendix A.

Service chiefs are among the most expensive positions for which we estimated annual costs. These costs are driven by the number of support staff associated with these positions. Other major contributors to the large cost estimates are required PSDs and the use of military aircraft for travel.

Costs of G/FOs by Position Category

Table 4.3 presents the support staff associated with O-7 G/FOs in the Army (brigadier general) by type of position. This is intended as an example of the average annual

Table 4.1
Support Staff for Select G/FOs Requiring Daily Protection

Position	Aide-de-Camp	Enlisted Aide	Other Personal	Executive Officer	Civilian Adminis-trative Assistant	Enlisted Executive Assistant	Protocol[a]	CAG[a]	Overall
CJCS	1.0	3.0	0.0	4.0	1.0	2.0	9.0	9.0	29.0
Chief of Naval Operations	1.0	3.0	0.0	3.0[b]	0.0[b]	7.0	2.0[b]	8.0[b]	24.0[c]
Chief of Staff of the Air Force	1.0	4.0	0.0	2.0	0.0	3.0	8.0	2.0[d]	20.0[c]
Chief of Staff, United States Army	1.0	4.0	0.0	4.0	1.0	4.0	9.0	7.0	30.0
Commandant of the Marine Corps	2.0	3.0	0.0	2.0	0.0	4.0	8.0	10.0	29.0

NOTES: Estimated values use manning documents reflecting the end of FY 2018. Table reflects averages in this service by position category based on these manning documents and applying a common support staff categorization with adjustments for consistency because of differences in service or joint organizations manning document terminology and structure.
[a] Many senior leadership positions share their protocol and CAG staff with other senior leaders. For example, protocol staff in the Army Chief of Staff's manning document support all of the Army senior leadership consisting of the Secretary of the Army, Under Secretary of the Army, Chief of Staff of the Army, Vice Chief of Staff of the Army, administrative assistant to the Secretary of the Army, the Director of the Army Staff, and Sergeant Major of the Army. To be consistent across the services and joint duty assignments, we have allocated these staff to the most senior position in the unit's manning document.
[b] Manning documents for the Navy exclude civilians.
[c] These totals are missing some staff support categories and would increase if more data became available.
[d] The manning document of the Air Force staff specifically states that a majority of the CAG supports the Secretary of the Air Force.

total cost of G/FOs by position category. For O-7 GOs, the amount of support staff is limited. G/FO positions with more-direct command authority, such as commanders, are authorized additional support, usually in some combination of personal and positional staff. Deputy director and chief of staff positions have notably less staff. Variation in support by position category is common across the services.

Table 4.4 presents the position-specific annual cost estimates averaged by service, grade, and position category. Rows with position category of "all" indicate the typical cost for that service and grade combination, regardless of position. A complete list of cost estimates for G/FOs by service, grade, and position category is available in Table A.3 in Appendix A.

Our G/FO cost estimates exhibit considerable variability by position type. Commanders have higher costs, driven by their increased support staff numbers, than G/FOs serving in G/FO staff positions. Much of this difference is in personal staff,

Table 4.2
Annual Total Costs (in Thousands) for Select G/FOs Requiring Daily Protection

Position	G/FO Direct Cost	Staff Direct (Personal)[a]	Staff Direct (Pos)	G/FO Train	G/FO Travel	Staff Travel	G/FO MILAIR	G/FO PSD	G/FO Quarters	Total
CJCS	$335	$669	$5,613	$5	$87	$922	$8,495	$3,779	$187	$20,092
Chief of Naval Operation	$340	$656	$4,333[b]	$3	$54	$280[b]	$3,886[c]	$831	$105	$10,488[d]
Chief of Staff of the Air Force	$346	$834	$2,870[e]	$5	$50	$27	$4,086	$1,087	$158	$9,463[d]
Chief of Staff, United States Army	$353	$855	$4,782	$8	$35	$130	$3,686	$3,957	$182	$13,989
Commandant of the Marine Corps	$339	$878	$4,750	$5	f	f	$3,886[c]	$1,238	$159	$11,255[d]

NOTES: Table reflects specific position estimates based on our application of the cost-estimating framework based on the manning documents provided by the services and DMDC. Estimated values in 2018 dollars. Caution should be used when comparing across ranks, as compositional differences in location, nature of position, organizational type, and functional area could drive cost differences.
[a] Direct costs of security personnel for G/FOs requiring continuous support are associated with the column "G/FO PSD."
[b] Manning documents for the Navy exclude civilians.
[c] Commandant of the Marine Corps and the Chief of Naval Operations are not represented in available MILAIR data, so we assumed similar usage as other service chiefs.
[d] These totals are missing some cost categories and would increase if more data became available.
[e] The Chief of Staff of the Air Force shares his or her CAG with the Secretary of the Air Force, which, by the support staff association rules outlined in Appendix B, leads the majority of the CAG to be assigned to the Secretary.
[f] We are not currently able to link Marine Corps service member travel costs to Marine Corps G/FOs.

with commanders and deputy or vice commanders having an average of one personal staff, generally an aide-de-camp, while other G/FO positions of this grade have little to no personal support staff.

Costs of G/FOs by Organization Type

Table 4.5 presents the support staff associated with O-7 GOs in the Army by organization type. This is intended as an example of the average annual total cost of G/FOs by organization type. G/FO positions leading larger organizations, such as operating forces or major commands, are authorized greater support. Headquarters staff positions have notably less staff. Variation in support by organization type is common across the services.

Table 4.3
Support Staff by Position Category for Army Brigadier Generals

Position Type	Aide-de-Camp	Enlisted Aide	Other Personal	Executive Officer	Civilian Adminis-trative Assistant	Enlisted Executive Assistant	Protocol	CAG	Overall
All	0.4	0.1	0.3	0.3	0.4	0.1	0.3	0.2	2.1
Chief of staff	0.0	0.0	0.0	0.0	0.0	1.0	0.0	0.0	1.0
Commander	0.7	0.1	0.4	0.4	0.5	0.2	0.7	0.3	3.3
Deputy director	0.0	0.0	0.0	0.0	0.0	0.0	0.0	0.0	0.0
Deputy or vice commander	0.6	0.0	0.4	0.2	0.2	0.0	0.0	0.1	1.5
Director	0.0	0.0	0.0	0.3	0.3	0.0	0.0	0.0	0.9
General/flag staff	0.0	0.0	0.0	0.6	0.0	0.0	0.0	0.0	0.6
PEO/deputy PEO	0.2	0.0	0.0	0.2	1.2	0.0	0.0	0.8	2.4

NOTES: Estimated values use manning documents reflecting the end of FY 2018. Table reflects averages in this service by position category based on these manning documents and applying a common support staff categorization with adjustments for consistency because of differences in service or joint organizations' manning document terminology and structure.

Table 4.6 presents position-specific annual total costs averaged by service, grade, and organization category. Rows with position category of "all" indicate the typical cost for that service and grade combination regardless of organization. A complete list of cost estimates for G/FOs by service, grade, and organization type is available in Table A.4 in Appendix A.

Similar to the costs for G/FOs grouped by position, we find considerable variation in our average annual cost estimates between Army brigadier generals based on the organization type. These cost estimates reflect differences in size of authorized support staff. G/FOs serving in the operating force have the highest personal support costs at $237,000 per year. In contrast, G/FOs serving in service chief of staff headquarters organizations have no personal support staff and average 0.8 staff for positional support. Also visible in this table is the variance in G/FO direct costs by location. Army brigadier generals' direct costs vary by location. Service chief of staff headquarters and service secretariat positions, located in Washington, D.C., have higher costs than generals in the operating force, which are more distributed geographically. However, headquarters and service secretariat positions show lower average travel costs, between $16,000 and

Table 4.4
Position-Specific Average Annual Total Costs (in Thousands) by Position Category for Army Brigadier Generals

Position Type	G/FO Count	G/FO Direct Cost	Staff Direct (Personal)	Staff Direct (Positional)	G/FO Train	G/FO Travel	Staff Travel	G/FO Quarters	Total
All	101	$289	$114	$181	$8	$39	$10	$1	$641
Chief of staff	2	$296	$0	$145	$8	$37	$0	$0	$486
Commander	43	$286	$184	$276	$8	$48	$15	$0	$816
Deputy director	2	$300	$0	$0	$8	$8	$0	$0	$316
Deputy or vice commander	19	$286	$158	$72	$8	$30	$6	$0	$561
Director	23	$292	$18	$115	$8	$24	$6	$4	$467
General/flag staff	7	$291	$0	$122	$8	$50	$6	$0	$476
PEO/deputy PEO	5	$292	$41	$252	$8	a	a	$0	$593[a]

NOTES: Average total cost estimates of specific G/FO positions. Total cost estimates are based on our application of the cost-estimating framework discussed in Chapter Two to the positions identified from manning documents provided for this study. Estimated values in 2018 dollars. G/FO positions are categorized based on Harrington et al. (2018).
[a] These totals are missing some cost categories and would increase if more data became available.

$31,000, while G/FOs in the operating force or a service component command have travel costs between $39,000 and $64,000.

Costs of G/FOs by Functional Area

Table 4.7 presents the support staff associated with O-7 GOs in the Army by functional area, intended as an example of the average annual total cost of G/FOs by functional area. G/FO positions involved in personnel-intensive activities, such as military operations, education, training, and logistics, are authorized greater support. Variation in support by functional area is common across the services.

Table 4.8 presents the position-specific annual total costs averaged by service, grade, and functional area. Rows with position category of "all" indicate the typical cost for that service and grade combination regardless of function. A complete list of cost estimates for G/FOs by service, grade, and functional area is available in Table A.5 in Appendix A.

We find considerable variation in our average annual cost estimates based on the functional area of the G/FO position. Notably, Army O-7s associated with force management, development, education, and training have an average of four staff

Table 4.5
Support Staff by Organization Type for Army Brigadier Generals

Organization Type	Aide-de-Camp	Enlisted Aide	Other Personal	Executive Officer	Civilian Adminis-trative Assistant	Enlisted Executive Assistant	Protocol	CAG	Overall
All	0.4	0.1	0.3	0.3	0.4	0.1	0.3	0.2	2.1
Combatant command	0.0	0.0	0.0	0.0	0.0	0.0	0.0	0.0	0.0
Direct reporting and similar[a]	0.5	0.1	0.2	0.4	0.7	0.0	0.2	0.3	2.3
Major and service commands	0.5	0.3	0.4	0.3	0.6	0.0	0.8	0.4	3.2
Operating forces	0.9	0.0	0.7	0.1	0.2	0.4	0.5	0.1	2.8
Service chief staff headquarters	0.0	0.0	0.0	0.5	0.1	0.1	0.0	0.1	0.8
Service component command	0.2	0.0	0.1	0.2	0.2	0.2	0.2	0.2	1.1
Service secretariat	0.0	0.0	0.0	0.7	0.3	0.0	0.0	0.0	1.0

NOTES: Estimated values use manning documents reflecting the end of FY 2018. Reflects averages in this service by position category based on these manning documents and applying a common support staff categorization with adjustments for consistency because of differences in service or joint organizations' manning document terminology and structure.
[a] "Direct reporting and similar" include direct reporting units, shore-based bureaus, acquisition activities, supporting establishments, and field operating agencies.

split between personal and positional. Other functional areas with above-average costs include materiel and logistics positions. On the other end of the spectrum are manpower and personnel positions and others with very few support staff.

Interpretation and Limitations

There is considerable cost variation in each cost category by rank, nature of position, organization, and function. Positional staff varies by position type and function, with commanders and operating force G/FOs having more personal staff while such positions as G/FO staff have more positional staff. This suggests that the marginal cost savings if a G/FO position were removed or reduced in rank would vary based on position category, organization type, and functional area.

Table 4.6
Position-Specific Average Annual Total Costs (in Thousands) by Organization Type for Army Brigadier Generals

Organization Type	G/FO Count	G/FO Direct Cost	Staff Direct (Personal)	Staff Direct (Position)	G/FO Train	G/FO Travel	Staff Travel	G/FO Quarters	Total
All	101	$289	$114	$181	$8	$39	$10	$1	$641
Combatant command	1	$276	$0	$0	$8	a	a	$0	$283[a]
Direct reporting and similar[b]	39	$290	$113	$212	$8	$44	$12	$0	$678
Major and service commands	12	$282	$163	$226	$8	$41	$0	$0	$719
Operating forces	19	$284	$237	$164	$8	$46	$18	$0	$757
Service chief staff headquarters	14	$297	$0	$151	$8	$27	$4	$6	$494
Service component command	13	$287	$52	$114	$8	$29	$10	$0	$500
Service secretariat	3	$300	$0	$190	$8	$13	$3	$0	$513

NOTES: Table reflects average total cost estimates of specific G/FO positions. Total cost estimates are based on our application of the cost-estimating framework discussed in Chapter Two to the positions identified from manning documents provided for this study. Estimated values in 2018 dollars. G/FO positions are categorized based on Harrington et al. (2018).
[a] These totals are missing some cost categories and would increase if more data became available.
[b] "Direct reporting and similar" include direct reporting units, shore-based bureaus, acquisition activities, supporting establishments, and field operating agencies.

High-ranking G/FOs with security details and authorized MILAIR travel have considerably higher costs. These costs are driven by the expensive nature of government air travel combined with extensive travel requirements for many of these positions and the considerable positional staff costs associated with G/FOs managing large organizations.

Table 4.7
Support Staff by Functional Category for Army Brigadier Generals

Functional Area	Aide-de-Camp	Enlisted Aide	Other Personal	Executive Officer	Civilian Administrative Assistant	Enlisted Executive Assistant	Protocol	CAG	Overall
All	0.4	0.1	0.3	0.3	0.4	0.1	0.3	0.2	2.1
Acquisition/ R&D	0.4	0.0	0.1	0.2	0.9	0.0	0.3	0.3	2.2
C4I	0.0	0.0	0.0	1.0	0.0	0.0	0.0	0.0	1.0
CD&I	0.2	0.0	0.0	0.6	0.2	0.0	0.0	0.0	1.0
Engineer	0.0	0.0	0.0	0.0	0.0	0.0	0.0	0.0	0.0
FMET	0.6	0.3	0.5	0.4	0.7	0.0	1.0	0.6	4.0
Manpower and personnel	0.0	0.0	0.0	0.3	0.3	0.3	0.0	0.0	1.0
Materiel and logistics	0.8	0.0	0.8	0.2	0.2	0.7	0.0	0.0	2.7
Military operations	0.7	0.0	0.4	0.1	0.1	0.2	0.0	0.0	1.5
Other	0.0	0.0	0.0	0.0	0.0	0.7	0.0	0.0	0.7
Program and financial management	0.0	0.0	0.0	0.0	0.5	0.0	0.0	0.0	0.5
Special staff	0.3	0.0	0.0	0.6	0.4	0.0	0.1	0.0	1.4
Strategic plans and policy	0.0	0.0	0.0	0.5	0.0	0.0	0.0	0.0	0.5

NOTES: Estimated values use manning documents reflecting the end of FY 2018. Reflects averages in this service by position category based on these manning documents and applying a common support staff categorization with adjustments for consistency because of differences in service or joint organizations manning document terminology and structure. Special staff include legal, medical, public affairs, chaplain, and congressional affairs; manpower includes personnel functions as well. R&D = research and development; CD&I = capabilities development/integration; FMET = force management, development, education, and training.

Table 4.8
Position-Specific Average Annual Total Costs (in Thousands) by Functional Area for Army
Brigadier Generals

Functional Area	G/FO Count	G/FO Direct Cost	Staff Direct (Personal)	Staff Direct (Positional)	G/FO Training	G/FO Travel	Staff Travel	G/FO Quarters	Total
All	101	$289	$114	$181	$8	$39	$10	$1	$641
Acquisition/ R&D	14	$289	$81	$187	$8	$27	$20	$0	$612
C4I	1	$281	$0	$160	$8	$61	$1	$0	$512
CD&I	5	$290	$31	$151	$8	$32	$10	$0	$521
Engineer	4	$296	$0	$0	$8	$32	$0	$0	$336
FMET	24	$286	$191	$350	$8	$49	$5	$0	$889
Manpower and personnel	3	$281	$0	$155	$8	$78	$13	$0	$536
Materiel and logistics	6	$285	$236	$137	$8	$21	$13	$0	$700
Military operations	21	$286	$158	$71	$8	$41	$16	$4	$585
Other	3	$292	$0	$97	$8	$40	$0	$0	$436
Program and financial management	2	$300	$0	$50	$8	$8	$0	$0	$365
Special staff	16	$292	$56	$186	$8	$33	$8	$0	$582
Strategic plans and policy	2	$300	$0	$111	$8	$1	$1	$0	$421

NOTES: Reflects average total cost estimates of specific G/FO positions. Total cost estimates are based on our application of the cost-estimating framework discussed in Chapter Two to the positions identified from manning documents provided for this study. Estimated values in 2018 dollars. G/FO positions are categorized based on Harrington et al. (2018). Special staff include legal, medical, public affairs, chaplain, and congressional affairs; manpower includes personnel functions.

CHAPTER FIVE

Summary and Recommendations

This report develops and applies a framework to estimate the costs of G/FOs and their support personnel. This cost-estimating framework is consistent with the requirement of section 596 of the 2019 NDAA and the recommendations of OSD, CAPE (2017b). We estimate average annual total costs of typical G/FOs as well as the annual total costs of specific G/FO positions. When estimating typical G/FO costs, we consider the direct costs (e.g., direct compensation, deferred compensation, benefits) of G/FOs and their support personnel and training costs using CAPE's FCoM model. When estimating position-specific costs, we include these same cost elements, as well as position-specific allowances, average annual travel costs of G/FOs serving in those positions, their support personnel who travel with them, the average cost of the G/FO quarters should the cost of those quarters consistently exceed BAH, and the cost of PSDs for those positions receiving continuous security. Prior to summarizing typical and specific G/FO cost estimates, we highlight key limitations and note appropriate interpretation and use of these cost estimates.

There are three fundamental limitations, discussed in Chapter Two, in estimating G/FO costs consistent with section 596 of the 2019 NDAA and OSD, CAPE (2017b). First, the existing data systems that we accessed were unable to directly link a person to an authorized position.[1] This limited the association of travel costs (which are person specific) to a specific G/FO position. We addressed this limitation by extracting travel records for G/FOs and staff in G/FOs' units that were near in grade to authorized support positions and included only costs for potential support whose travel was concurrent with a G/FO. Although this allowed us to associate travel costs in most cases, G/FO positions in which there are multiple G/FOs of the same grade in the same unit were still likely to be under- or overestimated as result (e.g., the chief and vice chief of staff of the Army are in the same UIC and are both O-10s, so we could not separate which persons were filling these O-10 positions). Second, existing data systems for tracking authorized positions vary across the services, and joint duty

---

[1] Each service can identify personnel filling a specific position. To ensure timely and consistent implementation of the cost-estimating framework discussed in Chapter Two, we determined that we would do data links and analysis.

assignments make it difficult to categorize support staff positions and associate them with a G/FO position. We addressed this limitation by developing a consistent method of categorizing support positions and associating them with specific G/FO positions (see Appendix B). Although this allowed us to consistently categorize and associate most positions with a G/FO, G/FO costs are still likely to be underestimated if G/FO support positions are not recorded on manning documents (e.g., joint positions in non-DoD government agencies; G/FO positions who use support staff authorized on a subordinate unit's manning document). Finally, existing data systems are subject to user input error, which limited our ability to identify whether positions are authorized and filled. We addressed this limitation by using information from other sources (e.g., service and joint G/FO management offices) to validate and correct the positions authorized at the end of FY 2018. Additionally, we collected joint manning documents from FY 2013 to FY 2018 to capture positions filled by G/FOs and G/FO support staff from different services. Although this allowed us to capture the majority of G/FO positions and their support staff, joint positions are likely to have their support staff travel costs underestimated if the position's service-specific UICs were not filled in or consistently updated. In a few specific cases, in which whole units were reported as not authorized in the manning documents (e.g., USFOR-A and the Joint Task Force for the Horn of Africa), our corrections could result in an overestimate of support staff as we compensated for this by assuming the entire unit was authorized. Consequently, we recommend caution when making comparisons across services or with joint positions. Differences in cost could reflect inconsistencies in reporting by organization.

Additionally, in Chapter One, we discussed how to interpret and use these cost estimates. Reflecting the congressional request in the 2019 NDAA, the G/FO costs estimates provided in this report are total costs of G/FO positions that are filled by a G/FO as of the end of FY 2018. Total costs, as defined, have limited utility for policy analysis because they lack a benchmark to compare against. Over time, if G/FO cost estimates are repeatedly produced, they can be used to assess trends in overall G/FO costs as well as specific G/FO cost elements. An alternative measure to total cost is marginal cost. A marginal cost measures the change in total cost because of a change in a factor that contributes to the cost. Marginal costs are used for comparative purposes and are often more appropriate measures in policy analysis—for example, if the policy under consideration is the cost savings associated with changing the authorized rank of a G/FO position or the cost savings associated with converting a G/FO position to SES. In a marginal analysis, it would be important to model how support positions are likely to change as a result of the change in the G/FO position (e.g., if a G/FO position is downgraded, the G/FO's officer aide position may remain the same, get downgraded, or get eliminated). More broadly, any policy analysis should also incorporate benefits of having a G/FO position, a factor not measured in this report.

When using the cost estimates provided in this report, it is important to note that G/FO positions vary in several key characteristics, including location, nature of position, organizational type, and function. G/FO positions by service may also vary along these positional characteristics as well. As discussed above, the data provided to identify and associate potential support staff with G/FOs varied by service. Although we tried to ensure comparable estimates, we document various cases where differences and inconsistencies in the data used for estimates may lead to under- or overestimated costs of one service relative to another. Understanding the differences in positional characteristics and data quality associated with a G/FO position's cost estimates is necessary and should be documented when using G/FO cost estimates in an analysis or reporting them in a publication.

Applying the cost-estimating framework described in Chapter Two, we find that the average annual total costs of a typical G/FO and his or her support staff increases with the G/FO rank. The cost increase primarily reflects an increase in positional support (i.e., personnel that support the G/FO's mission), and there is a smaller increase in costs because of personal support (i.e., personnel that support the G/FO's personal needs). Training costs, as represented by FCoM, reflect a service's annual cost of training averaged across its active-duty end strength and represent less than 2 percent of the typical G/FO position costs.

We find that costs of specific G/FO positions vary substantially by nature of position, organizational type, and function. Estimated costs range from $270,000 for O-7 G/FOs with no support to more than $10 million for O-10 G/FOs that receive continuous protection and are required to use government aircraft for official travel. High G/FO costs are primarily driven by the direct costs of supporting personnel and the cost of government air travel for personnel required to use it.

G/FO matters remain of great interest to Congress and are given routine attention in annual NDAAs. One of the original purposes for GAO (2014), a precursor to this report, was congressional interest in assessing trends in G/FO costs. If G/FO costs are estimated again in the future, there are several modifications to G/FO costing definitions, the costing approach, and how data are collected by DoD that would reduce the effort involved in estimating those costs and improve the measure's ability to reflect key differences in costs across specific G/FO positions.

Recommendations

We make nine recommendations aimed at improving and facilitating the estimation of G/FO costs, as defined in OSD, CAPE (2017b). These recommendations apply only if G/FO costs are to be estimated in the future.

The first five recommendations pertain to potential improvements in the G/FO costing definitions as approved in section 596 of the 2019 NDAA that would speed future estimation and improve the utility of G/FO costs estimates for policy analysis. The last four recommendations pertain to potential improvements that would facilitate data collection that could improve the accuracy of G/FO cost estimates. Some of these recommendations may require substantial coordination and cost. Consequently, DoD and Congress should consider the expected benefits of improving the accuracy of G/FO cost estimates relative to the expected cost of implementing these recommendations.

Recommendation 1: Develop a Framework for Estimating Marginal Costs

Now that G/FO costs have been estimated, it is reasonable to expect that stakeholders in Congress and DoD may want to use these cost estimates for policy analysis, such as justification for a G/FO position or for downgrading or eliminating a G/FO position. Point estimates of total cost, such as those presented in this report, may be incorrectly interpreted as potential cost savings from eliminating a G/FO's position or downgrading a G/FO position's authorized grade. Most of the estimated G/FO costs reflect position-specific costs, which are independent of the authorized grade. As discussed throughout this report, a marginal cost estimate would need to consider whether there is commensurate reduction in staff and/or staff rank. For example, the cost of a hypothetical Air Force O-9 position with an O-5 as an executive officer located in the Washington, D.C., area is estimated to be $588,000. Downgrading this hypothetical position to an O-8 with no change in support staff would reduce costs by $13,000. Reducing the pay grade of the executive officer support position would reduce the cost of the G/FO position by an additional $25,000. In this example, the total reduction in costs from reducing the GO and his or her support by a grade is estimated to be approximately $38,000 or 6.5 percent.[2]

We recommend extending the cost-estimating framework developed in this report to include an approach for analyzing the marginal cost associated with changing a G/FO position's authorized grade. This framework should incorporate the cost implications of proposed changes based on a specific G/FO position's service, organizational type, function, and positional category.

Recommendation 2: Exclude G/FO Official Residence Costs from Future G/FO Cost Estimates of Specific G/FO Positions

G/FO official residences are not always tied to a specific G/FO position. Service-owned and privately leased quarters are reported annually as part of the "General and Flag Officer Quarters" budget exhibit if they exceed $35,000 for government-owned facilities and $50,000 for privately leased quarters. Most G/FO quarters do not have regular O&M budgets exceeding G/FO BAH costs, which are approximately $39,000 annually for O-7 G/FOs. Instances when G/FO quarters exceed BAH are generally isolated to once or twice in a five- to ten-year window, suggesting that these costs are

---

[2] The small reduction in cost associated with going from an O-9 to O-8 is because of salary caps. Grades above O-8 are capped for most relevant years of service in the pay table. An analogous exercise going from a hypothetical O-8 position with an O-4 executive officer to an O-7 position with an O-3 executive officer would be estimated to reduce G/FO position costs by 11.5 percent.

associated with periodic renovations rather than continually high operating costs for most G/FO quarters. More-expensive homes may be categorized as historical residences, such as the Chief of Naval Operations' and the Commandant of Marines Corps' residences. In such cases, these residences would likely be kept up and maintained regardless of whether a specific G/FO resided there.

Because G/FO official residences are not always tied to specific positions, including them in G/FO-specific costs may lead to spurious changes in costs over time as G/FOs filling a specific G/FO position are assigned different G/FO residences. Additionally, an existing reporting requirement permits regular monitoring of cost trends for official residences. Consequently, we recommend excluding them in future cost estimates of specific G/FO positions. This recommendation is consistent with OSD, CAPE (2017b).

Recommendation 3: Exclude G/FO Training Costs as a Separate Cost Category in Future G/FO Cost Estimates

The 2019 NDAA required a separate cost category for G/FO training costs and required FCoM to estimate these costs. FCoM training costs reflect a service's total training costs reported in O&M annual budget requests divided by end strength. This value is not an accurate representation of G/FO-specific training. G/FOs receive G/FO-specific training, including CAPSTONE and PINNACLE provided by NDU, as well as service-specific training. If G/FO training costs are to be estimated, an ideal measure would account for G/FO-specific training provided by the NDU and other service and joint organization universities, colleges, and training centers.

These types of data are not routinely collected and reported for specific G/FO positions. Outside this G/FO cost effort, there would be no reason to do so. Based on NDU-only training costs, the annualized cost of G/FO-specific training does not exceed $10,000 (annualized over the expected duration of a G/FO's career). Investigation of Army, Navy, and Marine Corps G/FO training costs indicates service-specific G/FO training costs are likely not more than $10,000 in annualized costs by service. Combining service-specific and NDU training costs yields costs not exceeding $20,000, and a more accurate average estimate (if collected) is likely to be substantially less. For the average O-7, this cost is less than 7 percent of the G/FO's own direct costs. For the average unified combatant commander position, this would be less than 0.2 percent of his or her overall costs.

The small contribution of this cost category to overall G/FO cost estimates, particularly compared with such things as travel and staff costs, suggests to us that the burden of data collection outweighs the improvements in the precision of total G/FO cost estimates. Considering the cost of data collection relative to the magnitude of costs added to the estimate when including or excluding cost categories, we recommend excluding G/FO training costs as a separate cost category in future cost estimates of G/FO positions.

Recommendation 4: Exclude the Cost of Protection Detail Extraordinary Equipment from Future G/FO Cost Estimates of Specific G/FO Positions

OSD, CAPE (2017b) recommended including extraordinary equipment used for security details. Equipment purchases are typically done for the PPO and may cover multiple protective details, including common equipment for principals who are not G/FOs. This makes it difficult to associate this cost element to a specific G/FO's detail. Additionally, equipment lasts for many years, making it difficult to track consistently across protection details and PPOs.

As noted in Chapter Two, these data were difficult to collect, and the data varied considerably by PPO. Ultimately, we estimated a $35,000 cost to each detail, reflecting an average across PPOs and excluding cost outliers. The estimated average total cost of a G/FO requiring continuous protection is $10 million, so the equipment cost is less than 0.4 percent of these G/FO position's costs.

The small contribution of these costs to overall G/FO cost estimates, particularly compared with such things as travel and staff costs, suggests to us that the burden of data collection outweighs the improvements in the precision of total G/FO cost estimates. Considering the cost of data collection relative to the magnitude of costs added to the estimate when including or excluding cost categories, we recommend excluding estimates of the cost of protection detail extraordinary equipment in future cost estimates of specific G/FO positions.

Recommendation 5: Incorporate Tax Advantage into the Cost of G/FOs and Their Support Personnel in Future G/FO Cost Estimates

FCoM, which we used to estimate G/FO and support personnel's direct costs, does not account for the tax advantage of allowances or in-kind benefits. If Congress is concerned with the additional cost of G/FO positions, then it is appropriate to incorporate forgone tax revenues from nontaxed forms of compensation, as these are a cost burden to the U.S. Treasury. This is consistent with how GAO (2014) estimated G/FO compensation.

Preliminary estimates suggest that the tax advantage can range from 3.4 to 4.3 percent of basic pay and allowances in a less urban area (e.g., Camp Lejeune) to 5.1 to 6.7 percent of basic pay and allowances in an urban area (e.g., Arlington, Virginia). The addition of the tax advantage is a relatively straightforward addition to future cost analyses, as it is based on federal tax formulas, which are common to all service members. Consequently, we recommend including the tax advantage of allowances or in-kind benefits in future cost estimates of typical and specific G/FO positions.

Recommendation 6 (for DoD): Collect Data That Link Specific Personnel to Their Authorized Position and Include in a Common Data System

A major limitation for consistently estimating specific G/FO costs was the inability of the study team to directly link a person to an authorized position. This is required to link travel costs, which current estimates suggest can be substantial, to specific G/FO positions. Although each service can identify personnel filling a specific position, to our knowledge and the knowledge of the research's sponsor, this capability is not available in a common data system available to the OSD.

To ensure consistent implementation, a single organization should link and analyze the data, so we do not believe it is a plausible alternative to have each service provide these data.

Existing personnel data, such as DMDC's active-duty master file, could incorporate information that would facilitate linking personnel to specific positions on service-manning documents across all services and joint duty assignments. In addition to benefiting future estimates of G/FO costs, linking specific positions to personnel could facilitate future research on DoD-wide human capital development, force structure, and retention behavior.

To facilitate future cost estimates of specific G/FO positions, we recommend that DoD collect data in a common data system that permits the linking of specific personnel to the authorized position those personnel are filling.

Recommendation 7 (for DoD): Develop Standardized Position Titles and Manning Document Structure Across the Services and Joint Organizations

A major limitation for consistently estimating specific G/FO costs was that systems for tracking authorized positions vary across the services and joint organizations. This affected the ability to consistently categorize support positions and associate them to a specific G/FO position. Manning documents are designed for service-specific usage, making broader comparisons across services difficult. Manning document categorizations are also not consistent across units within services or across joint duty assignments.

To facilitate future cost estimates of specific G/FO positions requiring consistent cross-service and within-service categorization, we recommend that DoD standardize position titles and the manning document structure across the services and for joint organizations.

Recommendation 8 (or Department of the Navy): Collect or Make Available Navy Civilian Manpower Authorizations in a Single Database to Facilitate Estimation of Civilian Support Costs

A limitation for consistently estimating specific G/FO costs for the Navy was that unit manpower authorizations provided for this study did not include civilian support staff. The Office of Navy Flag Officer Management, Distribution and Development stated that Navy civilian manpower authorizations are not accessible in a centralized location. Consequently, civilian support staff costs were imputed based on the other services. As civilians serve in support positions for G/FOs, a single database comprising civilian and military position authorizations by unit would support the efficient analysis of manpower requirements and improve the comparability of support staff estimates with the other services and joint duty assignments.

To facilitate future cost estimates of specific G/FO positions requiring consistent manning documentation for units led by G/FOs, we recommend that the Department of the Navy collect civilian manpower authorizations in a single database that will permit the affiliation of these staffs with the units they support and the military manpower also supporting these units.

Recommendation 9 (for DMDC): Collect UICs Reflecting the Unit a Service Member Is Assigned to in the Marine Corps and DEPTID for Joint Duty Assignments

Service manpower authorizations are by UIC. DMDC's active-duty master file collects primary, secondary, and duty unit identifier codes for each service member. In DMDC's personnel files, for all services except the Marine Corps, this corresponds to the UIC. In DMDC's personnel files, for the Marine Corps, this corresponds to a resource utilization code (RUC). Multiple RUCs exist for a specific UIC. Consequently, Marine Corps personnel cannot be consistently associated with the unique unit to which they are assigned using DMDC's personnel files.

Joint duty assignment authorizations are associated with DEPTID. DMDC personnel files do not collect this unit identifier. Additionally, service UICs are not consistently collected as part of manning documents for joint duty assignments (i.e., this field in DMDC's Fourth Estate Manpower Tracking System is an optional input). If a joint position can be filled by any service, then it may have at least one UIC for each service. Without DEPTID in the personnel records, or service UICs consistently recorded in joint unit manning documents, it is difficult to associate personnel with specific joint units.

To facilitate future cost estimates of specific G/FO positions requiring person-specific records (e.g., travel), we recommend DMDC collect the Marine Corps' UICs for the Marine Corps personnel and DEPTID for joint duty assignments.

G/FO Cost Estimates for Specific Positions

This appendix presents complete lists of (1) support staff for G/FOs requiring continuous PSDs or government air travel (Table A.1); (2) annual cost estimates for G/FOs requiring continuous PSDs or government air travel (Table A.2); (3) cost estimates for G/FOs by service, grade, and position category (Table A.3); cost estimates for G/FOs by service, grade, and organization type (Table A.4); and cost estimates by service, grade, and functional area (Table A.5). See Chapter Four for a discussion of these categories.

Table A.1
Support Staff for Select G/FOs Requiring Daily Protection or Required to Use Government Air Travel for Official Business

Position	Aide-de-camp	Enlisted Aide	Other Personal	Executive Officer	Civilian Admin	Enlisted Executive Assistant	Protocol[a]	CAG[a]	Total
Chairman of the Joint Chiefs of Staff	1.0	3.0	0.0	4.0	1.0	2.0	9.0	9.0	29.0
Vice Chairman of the Joint Chiefs of Staff	1.0	3.0	0.0	2.0	0.0	2.0	0.0	1.0	9.0
Chief of Naval Operations	1.0	3.0	0.0	3.0[b]	0.0[b]	7.0	2.0[b]	8.0[b]	24.0[c]
Chief of Staff of the Air Force	1.0	4.0	0.0	2.0	0.0	3.0	8.0	2.0[d]	20.0[c]
Chief of Staff, U.S. Army	1.0	4.0	0.0	4.0	1.0	4.0	9.0	7.0	30.0
Commandant of the Marine Corps	2.0	3.0	0.0	2.0	0.0	4.0	8.0	10.0	29.0
Chief, National Guard Bureau	1.0	2.0	0.0	2.0	1.0	1.0	0.0	0.0	7.0

Table A.1—Continued

Position	Aide-de-camp	Enlisted Aide	Other Personal	Executive Officer	Civilian Admin	Enlisted Executive Assistant	Protocol[a]	CAG[a]	Total
Commander, U.S. Africa Command	1.0	2.0	1.0	1.0	0.0	0.0	0.0	4.0	9.0
Commander, U.S. Central Command	1.0	2.0	1.0	3.0	0.0	2.0	6.0	3.0	18.0
Commander, U.S. Cyber Command; Director, National Security Agency	0.0[e]	2.0	0.0	1.0	0.0	0.0	6.0	0.0	9.0[c]
Commander, U.S. European Command; Supreme Allied Commander, Europe	0.0[e]	2.0	0.0	2.0	1.0	1.0	7.0	0.0	13.0[c]
Commander, U.S. Indo-Pacific Command	2.0	2.0	2.0	3.0	0.0	8.0	9.0	4.0	30.0
Commander, U.S. Northern Command; Commander, North American Aerospace Defense Command	1.0	2.0	0.0	2.0	1.0	0.0	7.0	2.0	15.0
Commander, U.S. Southern Command	1.0	2.0	2.0	2.0	0.0	6.0	2.0	1.0	16.0
Commander, U.S. Special Operations Command	0.0[e]	2.0	1.0	1.0	1.0	5.0	8.0	2.0	20.0[c]
Commander, U.S. Strategic Command	1.0	2.0	0.0	2.0	1.0	2.0	11.0	7.0	26.0
Commander, U.S. Transportation Command	1.0	2.0	1.0	2.0	1.0	0.0	5.0	2.0	14.0

Table A.1—Continued

Position	Aide-de-camp	Enlisted Aide	Other Personal	Executive Officer	Civilian Admin	Enlisted Executive Assistant	Protocol[a]	CAG[a]	Total
Commander, Resolute Support Mission, NATO; Commander, USFOR-A	1.0	2.0	1.0	1.0	0.0	1.0	0.0	0.0	6.0
Commander, United Nations Command; Commander, Combined Forces Command; Commander, USFK	1.0	2.0	1.0	1.0	0.0	1.0	2.0	0.0	8.0
Commander, U.S. Naval Forces Central Command	0.0[e]	1.0	0.0	1.0[b]	0.0[b]	1.0	0.0[b]	1.0[b]	4.0[c]
Commander, U.S. Naval Forces Europe/Africa; Commander, Allied Joint Forces Command, Naples	0.0[e]	3.0	0.0	0.0[b]	0.0[b]	0.0	0.0[b]	0.0[b]	3.0[c]
Commander, U.S. Air Forces in Europe/Africa; Commander, Allied Air Command	1.0	1.0	0.0	0.0	1.0	0.0	4.0	2.0	9.0

NOTES: Estimated values use manning documents reflecting the end of FY 2018. Table reflects averages in this service by position category based on these manning documents and applying a common support staff categorization with adjustments for consistency because of differences in service or joint organizations' manning document terminology and structure.

[a] Many senior leadership positions share their protocol and CAG staff with other senior leaders. For example, protocol staff in the Army Chief of Staff's manning document support all of the Army senior leadership consisting of the Secretary of the Army, Under Secretary of the Army, Chief of Staff of the Army, Vice Chief of Staff of the Army, administrative assistant to the Secretary of the Army, Director of the Army Staff, and Sergeant Major of the Army. To be consistent across the services and joint duty assignments, we have allocated these staff to the most senior position in the unit's manning document.

[b] Manning documents for the Navy exclude civilians.

[c] These totals are missing some staff support categories and would increase if more data became available.

[d] The manning document of the Air Force staff specifically states that a majority of the CAG supports the Secretary of the Air Force.

[e] Reported number reflects unit manning document but are flagged as a likely underreported value as such senior positions typically have aides-de-camp.

Table A.2
Annual Total Costs (in Thousands) for Select G/FOs Requiring Daily Protection or Required to Use Government Air Travel for Official Business

Position	G/FO Direct Cost	Staff Direct-Personal[a]	Staff Direct-Positional	G/FO Training	G/FO Travel	Staff Travel[b]	G/FO MILAIR	G/FO PSD	G/FO Quarters	Total
Chairman of the Joint Chiefs of Staff	$335	$669	$5,613	$5	$87	$922	$8,495	$3,779	$187	$20,092
Vice Chairman of the Joint Chiefs of Staff	$342	$684	$1,127	$5	$87	$922	$1,446	$4,429	$129	$9,172
Chief of Naval Operations	$340	$656	$4,333[c]	$3	$54	$280[c]	$3,886[d]	$831	$105	$10,488[e]
Chief of Staff of the Air Force	$346	$834	$2,870[f]	$5	$50	$27	$4,086	$1,087	$158	$9,463[e]
Chief of Staff, U.S. Army	$353	$855	$4,782	$8	$35	$130	$3,686	$3,957	$182	$13,989
Commandant of the Marine Corps	$339	$878	$4,750	$5	[d]	[d]	$3,886[d]	$1,238	$159	$11,255[e]
Chief, National Guard Bureau	$342	$518	$800	$5	[g]	[g]	$3,185	$1,326	$0	$6,176[e]
Commander, U.S. Africa Command	$310	$660	$1,115	$5	$52	$118	$9,561	$3,141	$0	$14,963
Commander, U.S. Central Command	$341	$646	$2,757	$5	$82	$1,159	$4,956	$1,950	$0	$11,897
Commander, U.S. Cyber Command; Director, National Security Agency	$330	$286[h]	$1,210	$5	$6	$0	$5,530	$0	$0	$7,368[e]
Commander, U.S. European Command; Supreme Allied Commander, Europe	$324	$314[h]	$2,146	$5	$24	$17	$7,862	$3,141	$0	$13,833[e]
Commander, U.S. Indo-Pacific Command	$344	$984	$4,212	$5	[g]	[g]	$7,677	$933	$116	$14,271[e]

Table A.2—Continued

Position	G/FO Direct Cost	Staff Direct-Personal[a]	Staff Direct-Positional	G/FO Training	G/FO Travel	Staff Travel[b]	G/FO MILAIR	G/FO PSD	G/FO Quarters	Total
Commander, U.S. Northern Command; Commander, North American Aerospace Defense Command	$327	$473	$2,083	$5	$19	$52	$3,996	$506	$0	$7,461[e]
Commander, U.S. Southern Command	$340	$820	$2,270	$5	$26	$46	$4,452	$3,362	$0	$11,320
Commander, U.S. Special Operations Command	$341	$434[h]	$2,911	$5	$73	$373	$5,624	$1,759	$0	$11,519[e]
Commander, U.S. Strategic Command	$328	$468	$3,821	$5	$39	$105	$4,654	$898	$0	$10,318
Commander, U.S. Transportation Command	$334	$596	$1,645	$5	$19	$21	$2,548	$644	$0	$5,812
Commander, Resolute Support Mission, NATO; Commander, USFOR-A	$349	$659	$399	$5	[g]	[g]	$4,750	$0	$0	$6,161[e]
Commander, United Nations Command; Commander, Combined Forces Command; Commander, USFK	$349	$695	$792	$5	[g]	[g]	$5,761	$2,767	$0	$10,368[e]
Commander, U.S. Naval Forces Central Command	$319	$155[h]	$807[c]	$3	$19	$26[c]	$0	$2,258	$223	$3,809[e]

Table A.2—Continued

Position	G/FO Direct Cost	Staff Direct-Personal[a]	Staff Direct-Positional	G/FO Training	G/FO Travel	Staff Travel[b]	G/FO MILAIR	G/FO PSD	G/FO Quarters	Total
Commander, U.S. Naval Forces Europe/ Africa; Commander, Allied Joint Forces Command, Naples	$328	$462[h]	$575[c]	$3	$26	$0[c]	$0	$167	$114	$1,675[e]
Commander, U.S. Air Forces in Europe/ Africa; Commander, Allied Air Command	$319	$364	$1,147	$5	$111	$111	$0	$1,530	$0	$3,586[e]

NOTES: Table reflects specific position estimates based on our application of the cost-estimating framework based on the manning documents provided by the services and DMDC. Estimated values in 2018 dollars. Caution should be used when comparing across ranks as compositional differences in location, nature of position, organizational type, and functional area could drive cost differences.
[a] Direct costs of security personnel for G/FOs requiring continuous support are associated with the column "General or Flag Officer Security."
[b] We are not currently able to link Marine Corps service member travel costs to Marine Corps G/FOs.
[c] Manning documents for the Navy exclude civilians.
[d] The Commandant of the Marine Corps and the Chief of Naval Operations are not represented in available MILAIR data, assumed similar usage as other service chiefs.
[e] These totals are missing some cost categories and would increase if more data became available.
[f] The Chief of Staff of the Air Force shares his or her CAG with the Secretary of the Air Force, which, by the support staff association rules described in Appendix B, leads the majority of the CAG to be assigned to the Secretary.
[g] Missing data from DTMO.
[h] Reported number reflects costs estimated using manning documents but are flagged as a likely underreported value.

Table A.3
Average Annual Total Costs by Service, Grade, and Position Category

Service	Grade	Position Type	G/FO Count	G/FO Direct Cost	Staff Direct (Personal)[a]	Staff Direct (Positional)	G/FO Training	G/FO Travel	Staff Travel	G/FO MILAIR	G/FO PSD	G/FO Quarters	Total
Air Force	O-7	All	94	$282	$20	$335	$5	$30	$2	$0	$0	$0	$673
Air Force	O-7	Chief of staff	1	$270	$0	$2,053	$5	$2	$0	$0	$0	$0	$2,329
Air Force	O-7	Commander	23	$277	$36	$589	$5	$32	$4	$0	$0	$0	$944
Air Force	O-7	Deputy director	3	$288	$0	$72	$5	$45	$1	$0	$0	$0	$410
Air Force	O-7	Deputy/vice commander	13	$279	$53	$141	$5	$27	$1	$0	$0	$0	$505
Air Force	O-7	Director	49	$284	$0	$250	$5	$28	$0	$0	$0	$0	$567
Air Force	O-7	General/flag staff	2	$293	$0	$522	$5	$27	$0	$0	$0	$0	$846
Air Force	O-7	PEO/deputy PEO	3	$286	$106	$202	$5	$37	$2	$0	$0	$0	$638
Air Force	O-8	All	49	$321	$67	$589	$5	$29	$6	$0	$0	$0	$1,018
Air Force	O-8	Chief of staff	1	$337	$0	$356	$5	$4	$0	$0	$0	$0	$702
Air Force	O-8	Commander	18	$314	$160	$893	$5	$47	$13	$0	$0	$0	$1,432
Air Force	O-8	Deputy director	2	$328	$0	$444	$5	$49	$0	$0	$0	$0	$826
Air Force	O-8	Deputy/vice commander	5	$318	$85	$678	$5	$17	$2	$0	$0	$0	$1,105
Air Force	O-8	Director	21	$325	$0	$357	$5	$13	$3	$0	$0	$0	$702

Table A.3—Continued

Service	Grade	Position Type	G/FO Count	G/FO Direct Cost	Staff Direct (Personal)[a]	Staff Direct (Positional)	G/FO Training	G/FO Travel	Staff Travel	G/FO MILAIR	G/FO PSD	G/FO Quarters	Total
Air Force	O-8	General/flag staff	2	$328	$0	$336	$5	$54	$1	$0	$0	$0	$724
Air Force	O-9	All	28	$333	$140	$904	$5	$42	$12	$0	$0	$3	$1,439
Air Force	O-9	Commander	11	$324	$264	$1,219	$5	$31	$21	$0	$0	$3	$1,865
Air Force	O-9	Deputy director	1	$341	$148	$357	$5	$46	$6	$0	$0	$0	$903
Air Force	O-9	Deputy/vice commander	4	$328	$69	$405	$5	$50	$1	$0	$0	$0	$858
Air Force	O-9	Director	3	$341	$99	$544	$5	$119	$10	$0	$0	$21	$1,139
Air Force	O-9	General/flag staff	7	$341	$21	$644	$5	$29	$8	$0	$0	$0	$1,048
Air Force	O-9	Other	1	$341	$0	$1,709	$5	$1	$0	$0	$0	$0	$2,056
Air Force	O-9	PEO/deputy PEO	1	$350	$154	$2,069	$5	$38	$3	$0	$0	$0	$2,619
Air Force	O-10	All	9	$332	$460	$2,071	$5	$56	$47	$454	$291	$18	$3,733
Air Force	O-10	Commander	7	$329	$430	$2,118	$5	$61	$54	$0	$219	$0	$3,216
Air Force	O-10	General/flag staff	2	$344	$565	$1,904	$5	$41	$21	$2,043	$543	$79	$5,545
Army	O-7	All	101	$289	$114	$181	$8	$39	$10	$0	$0	$1	$641
Army	O-7	Chief of staff	2	$296	$0	$145	$8	$37	$0	$0	$0	$0	$486
Army	O-7	Commander	43	$286	$184	$276	$8	$48	$15	$0	$0	$0	$816

Table A.3—Continued

Service	Grade	Position Type	G/FO Count	G/FO Direct Cost	Staff Direct (Personal)[a]	Staff Direct (Positional)	G/FO Training	G/FO Travel	Staff Travel	G/FO MILAIR	G/FO PSD	G/FO Quarters	Total
Army	O-7	Deputy director	2	$300	$0	$0	$8	$8	$0	$0	$0	$0	$316
Army	O-7	Deputy/vice commander	19	$286	$158	$72	$8	$30	$6	$0	$0	$0	$561
Army	O-7	Director	23	$292	$18	$115	$8	$24	$6	$0	$0	$4	$467
Army	O-7	General/flag staff	7	$291	$0	$122	$8	$50	$6	$0	$0	$0	$476
Army	O-7	PEO/deputy PEO	5	$292	$41	$252	$8	b	b	$0	$0	$0	$593[c]
Army	O-7	All	82	$322	$203	$308	$8	$36	$20	$0	$0	$6	$903
Army	O-8	Chief of staff	1	$318	$0	$90	$8	$110	$146	$0	$0	$0	$671
Army	O-8	Commander	48	$319	$314	$362	$8	$43	$21	$0	$0	$3	$1,071
Army	O-8	Deputy director	2	$333	$0	$123	$8	$28	$1	$0	$0	$0	$494
Army	O-8	Deputy/vice commander	13	$325	$111	$220	$8	$21	$1	$0	$0	$15	$702
Army	O-8	Director	9	$329	$0	$199	$8	$27	$30	$0	$0	$0	$592
Army	O-8	General/flag staff	6	$327	$25	$345	$8	$21	$19	$0	$0	$29	$775
Army	O-8	PEO/deputy PEO	3	$326	$0	$255	$8	b	b	$0	$0	$0	$589[c]
Army	O-9	All	34	$342	$256	$624	$8	$34	$16	$0	$0	$33	$1,313

Table A.3—Continued

Service	Grade	Position Type	G/FO Count	G/FO Direct Cost	Staff Direct (Personal)[a]	Staff Direct (Positional)	G/FO Training	G/FO Travel	Staff Travel	G/FO MILAIR	G/FO PSD	G/FO Quarters	Total
Army	O-9	Commander	16	$337	$379	$586	$8	$44	$17	$0	$0	$38	$1,409
Army	O-9	Deputy/vice commander	5	$338	$219	$593	$8	$29	$25	$0	$0	$0	$1,212
Army	O-9	Director	3	$345	$212	$786	$8	$11	$1	$0	$0	$25	$1,389
Army	O-9	General/flag staff	10	$350	$91	$652	$8	$25	$14	$0	$0	$43	$1,183
Army	O-10	All	7	$342	$483	$1,624	$8	$38	$66	$527	$565	$50	$3,703
Army	O-10	Commander	5	$338	$431	$1,118	$8	$39	$41	$0	$0	$0	$1,975
Army	O-10	General/flag staff	2	$351	$615	$2,889	$8	$35	$130	$1,843	$1,979	$175	$8,024
Joint	O-7	All	110	$290	$14	$129	$5	$15	$1	$0	$0	$0	$454
Joint	O-7	Chief of staff	2	$300	$128	$493	$5	b	b	$0	$0	$0	$927[c]
Joint	O-7	Commander	9	$288	$44	$70	$5	$4	$0	$0	$0	$0	$411
Joint	O-7	Deputy director	43	$292	$0	$85	$5	$9	$0	$0	$0	$0	$392
Joint	O-7	Deputy/vice commander	12	$296	$44	$113	$5	$38	$2	$0	$0	$0	$499
Joint	O-7	Director	33	$288	$10	$132	$5	$15	$0	$0	$0	$0	$451
Joint	O-7	General/flag staff	9	$281	$0	$283	$5	$34	$3	$0	$0	$1	$607
Joint	O-7	Other	2	$296	$0	$317	$5	b	b	$0	$0	$0	$618[c]

Table A.3—Continued

Service	Grade	Position Type	G/FO Count	G/FO Direct Cost	Staff Direct (Personal)[a]	Staff Direct (Positional)	G/FO Training	G/FO Travel	Staff Travel	G/FO MILAIR	G/FO PSD	G/FO Quarters	Total
Joint	O-8	All	89	$322	$33	$220	$5	$29	$11	$0	$0	$5	$625
Joint	O-8	Chief of staff	11	$319	$0	$235	$5	$16	$7	$0	$0	$8	$599
Joint	O-8	Commander	11	$321	$156	$338	$5	$92	$30	$0	$0	$0	$942
Joint	O-8	Deputy director	15	$327	$0	$67	$5	$12	$4	$0	$0	$0	$415
Joint	O-8	Deputy/vice commander	4	$320	$84	$159	$5	$9	$0	$0	$0	$0	$578
Joint	O-8	Director	37	$323	$23	$258	$5	$29	$12	$0	$0	$5	$655
Joint	O-8	General/flag staff	9	$320	$0	$195	$5	$26	$8	$0	$0	$17	$560
Joint	O-8	PEO/deputy PEO	2	$314	$0	$181	$5	b	b	$0	$0	$0	$500[c]
Joint	O-9	All	40	$338	$106	$269	$5	$22	$7	$0	$0	$13	$761
Joint	O-9	Commander	4	$330	$116	$451	$5	$48	$0	$0	$0	$0	$951
Joint	O-9	Deputy director	4	$342	$37	$68	$5	b	b	$0	$0	$0	$452[c]
Joint	O-9	Deputy/vice commander	12	$332	$179	$278	$5	$26	$12	$0	$0	$9	$841
Joint	O-9	Director	16	$340	$84	$301	$5	$9	$1	$0	$0	$27	$769
Joint	O-9	General/flag staff	1	$350	$152	$519	$5	b	b	$0	$0	$0	$1,034[c]
Joint	O-9	Other	3	$345	$0	$0	$5	b	b	$0	$0	$0	$350[c]

Table A.3—Continued

Service	Grade	Position Type	G/FO Count	G/FO Direct Cost	Staff Direct (Personal)[a]	Staff Direct (Positional)	G/FO Training	G/FO Travel	Staff Travel	G/FO MILAIR	G/FO PSD	G/FO Quarters	Total
Joint	O-10	All	15	$336	$594	$2,194	$5	$47	$340	$5,366	$1,909	$29	$10,818
Joint	O-10	Commander	12	$335	$586	$2,113	$5	$38	$210	$5,614	$1,592	$10	$10,503
Joint	O-10	General/flag staff	3	$339	$624	$2,516	$5	$87	$922	$4,375	$3,178	$105	$12,150
Marines	O-7	All	22	$283	$184	$361	$5	$22[d]	$3[d]	$0	$0	$3	$860[c]
Marines	O-7	Commander	13	$279	$284	$337	$5	$29[d]	$2[d]	$0	$0	$1	$937[c]
Marines	O-7	Deputy/vice commander	1	$299	$353	$0	$5	$26[d]	$10[d]	$0	$0	$47	$740[c]
Marines	O-7	Director	5	$288	$0	$491	$5	$2[d]	$0[d]	$0	$0	$0	$786[c]
Marines	O-7	General/flag staff	3	$282	$0	$373	$5	$20[d]	$6[d]	$0	$0	$0	$686[c]
Marines	O-8	All	22	$309	$224	$229	$5	$61[d]	$6[d]	$0	$0	$3	$837[c]
Marines	O-8	Commander	17	$307	$284	$223	$5	$66[d]	$6[d]	$0	$0	$4	$894[c]
Marines	O-8	Deputy/vice commander	1	$314	$108	$225	$5	$56[d]	$6[d]	$0	$0	$0	$714[c]
Marines	O-8	Director	1	$313	$0	$601	$5	b	b	$0	$0	$0	$919[c]
Marines	O-8	General/flag staff	3	$319	$0	$140	$5	$10[d]	$0[d]	$0	$0	$0	$475[c]
Marines	O-9	All	15	$327	$355	$696	$5	$66[d]	$4[d]	$0	$0	$5	$1,458[c]
Marines	O-9	Chief of staff	1	$335	$213	$469	$5	b	b	$0	$0	$0	$1,021[c]
Marines	O-9	Commander	8	$324	$499	$491	$5	$81[d]	$5[d]	$0	$0	$6	$1,411[c]

Table A.3—Continued

Service	Grade	Position Type	G/FO Count	G/FO Direct Cost	Staff Direct (Personal)[a]	Staff Direct (Positional)	G/FO Training	G/FO Travel	Staff Travel	G/FO MILAIR	G/FO PSD	G/FO Quarters	Total
Marines	O-9	General/flag staff	6	$329	$188	$1,007	$5	$5[d]	$1[d]	$0	$0	$5	$1,539[c]
Marines	O-10	All	2	$337	$752	$2,902	$5	[b]	[b]	$1,943	$619	$91	$6,649[c]
Marines	O-10	General/flag staff	2	$337	$752	$2,902	$5	[b]	[b]	$1,943	$619	$91	$6,649[c]
Navy	O-7	All	74	$285	$92	$341[e]	$3	$38	$15[e]	$0	$0	$2	$775[c]
Navy	O-7	Commander	43	$282	$132	$397[e]	$3	$44	$22[e]	$0	$0	$2	$882[c]
Navy	O-7	Deputy director	4	$286	$0	$447[e]	$3	$15	$7[e]	$0	$0	$1	$759[c]
Navy	O-7	Deputy/vice commander	3	$286	$0	$208[e]	$3	$42	$2[e]	$0	$0	$0	$541[c]
Navy	O-7	Director	19	$291	$58	$271[e]	$3	$29	$8[e]	$0	$0	$2	$661[c]
Navy	O-7	General/flag staff	1	$283	$0	$232[e]	$3	$17	$0[e]	$0	$0	$0	$535[c]
Navy	O-7	PEO/deputy PEO	4	$290	$0	$85[e]	$3	$32	$0[e]	$0	$0	$0	$411[c]
Navy	O-8	All	42	$320	$90	$572[e]	$3	$24	$14[e]	$0	$0	$11	$1,033[c]
Navy	O-8	Commander	17	$315	$144	$613[e]	$3	$32	$24[e]	$0	$0	$14	$1,145[c]
Navy	O-8	Deputy director	1	$323	$456	$1,477[e]	$3	$9	$8[e]	$0	$0	$24	$2,300[c]
Navy	O-8	Deputy/vice commander	2	$328	$0	$363[e]	$3	$33	$5[e]	$0	$0	$12	$744[c]
Navy	O-8	Director	17	$322	$50	$594[e]	$3	$13	$9[e]	$0	$0	$8	$1,000[c]

Table A.3—Continued

Service	Grade	Position Type	G/FO Count	G/FO Direct Cost	Staff Direct (Personal)[a]	Staff Direct (Positional)[e]	G/FO Training	G/FO Travel	Staff Travel	G/FO MILAIR	G/FO PSD	G/FO Quarters	Total
Navy	O-8	General/flag staff	1	$323	$0	$530[e]	$3	[b]	[b, e]	$0	$0	$0	$856[c]
Navy	O-8	PEO/deputy PEO	4	$321	$0	$197[e]	$3	$31	$0[e]	$0	$0	$4	$556[c]
Navy	O-9	All	27	$333	$233	$931[e]	$3	$28	$26[e]	$0	$84	$41	$1,678[c]
Navy	O-9	Commander	15	$331	$294	$977[e]	$3	$29	$34[e]	$0	$151	$57	$1,876[c]
Navy	O-9	Deputy director	1	$336	$276	$927[e]	$3	$10	$3[e]	$0	$0	$9	$1,564[c]
Navy	O-9	Deputy/vice commander	1	$328	$341	$753[e]	$3	$12	$27[e]	$0	$0	$6	$1,470[c]
Navy	O-9	Director	4	$336	$140	$732[e]	$3	$41	$17[e]	$0	$0	$40	$1,309[c]
Navy	O-9	General/flag staff	6	$336	$118	$979[e]	$3	$22	$18[e]	$0	$0	$12	$1,487[c]
Navy	O-10	All	6	$335	$642	$2,009[e]	$3	$33	$123[e]	$648	$166	$101	$4,061[c]
Navy	O-10	Commander	3	$333	$540	$1,521[e]	$3	$22	$33[e]	$0	$56	$105	$2,614[c]
Navy	O-10	Director	1	$336	$509	$1,415[e]	$3	$22	$81[e]	$0	$0	$74	$2,441[c]
Navy	O-10	General/flag staff	2	$338	$862	$3,039[e]	$3	$54	$280[e]	$1,943	$416	$107	$7,042[c]

NOTES: Table reflects average total cost estimates of specific G/FO positions. Total cost estimates are based on our application of the cost-estimating framework discussed in Chapter Two to the positions identified from manning documents provided for this study. Estimated values in 2018 dollars. G/FO positions are categorized based on Harrington et al. (2018).

[a] Direct costs of security personnel for G/FOs requiring continuous support are associated with the column "General or Flag Officer Security."

[b] Missing data from DTMO.

[c] These totals are missing some cost categories and would increase if more data became available.

[d] We are not currently able to link all Marine Corps service member travel costs to Marine Corps G/FOs.

[e] Manning documents for the Navy exclude civilians.

Table A.4
Average Annual Total Costs by Service, Grade, and Organization Type

Service	Grade	Organization Type	G/FO Count	G/FO Direct Cost	Staff Direct (Personal)[a]	Staff Direct (Positional)	G/FO Training	G/FO Travel	Staff Travel	G/FO MILAIR	G/FO PSD	G/FO Quarters	Total
Air Force	O-7	All	94	$282	$20	$335	$5	$30	$2	$0	$0	$0	$673
Air Force	O-7	Defense, joint, or service agency	1	$293	$0	$217	$5	$2	$0	$0	$0	$0	$517
Air Force	O-7	Direct reporting and similar	18	$282	$40	$546	$5	$29	$6	$0	$0	$0	$907
Air Force	O-7	Major and service commands	27	$280	$20	$164	$5	$34	$0	$0	$0	$0	$503
Air Force	O-7	National	2	$293	$0	$0	$5	b	b	$0	$0	$0	$298[c]
Air Force	O-7	Operating forces	19	$275	$30	$323	$5	$33	$1	$0	$0	$0	$666
Air Force	O-7	Other	1	$282	$0	$802	$5	$28	$0	$0	$0	$0	$1,116
Air Force	O-7	Service chief staff headquarters	13	$292	$0	$335	$5	$22	$0	$0	$0	$0	$654
Air Force	O-7	Service component command	4	$271	$0	$872	$5	$33	$0	$0	$0	$0	$1,180
Air Force	O-7	Service secretariat	9	$293	$0	$250	$5	$24	$1	$0	$0	$0	$573
Air Force	O-8	All	49	$321	$67	$589	$5	$29	$6	$0	$0	$0	$1,018

Table A.4—Continued

Service	Grade	Organization Type	G/FO Count	G/FO Direct Cost	Staff Direct (Personal)[a]	Staff Direct (Positional)[a]	G/FO Training	G/FO Travel	Staff Travel	G/FO MILAIR	G/FO PSD	G/FO Quarters	Total
Air Force	O-8	Direct reporting and similar	8	$315	$126	$1,070	$5	$36	$11	$0	$0	$0	$1,563
Air Force	O-8	Major and service commands	10	$320	$42	$400	$5	$14	$1	$0	$0	$0	$781
Air Force	O-8	Operating forces	10	$313	$154	$658	$5	$56	$14	$0	$0	$0	$1,199
Air Force	O-8	Service chief staff headquarters	14	$327	$0	$354	$5	$20	$3	$0	$0	$0	$708
Air Force	O-8	Service component command	1	$314	$341	$1,045	$5	$12	$18	$0	$0	$0	$1,734
Air Force	O-8	Service secretariat	6	$328	$0	$624	$5	$24	$0	$0	$0	$0	$981
Air Force	O-9	All	28	$333	$140	$904	$5	$42	$12	$0	$0	$3	$1,439
Air Force	O-9	Defense, joint, or service agency	1	$341	$148	$0	$5	$151	$0	$0	$0	$64	$709
Air Force	O-9	Direct reporting and similar	5	$329	$273	$1,445	$5	$26	$17	$0	$0	$6	$2,100
Air Force	O-9	Major and service commands	6	$329	$164	$1,107	$5	$38	$3	$0	$0	$0	$1,646

Table A.4—Continued

Service	Grade	Organization Type	G/FO Count	G/FO Direct Cost	Staff Direct (Personal)[a]	Staff Direct (Positional)	G/FO Training	G/FO Travel	Staff Travel	G/FO MILAIR	G/FO PSD	G/FO Quarters	Total
Air Force	O-9	Operating forces	2	$316	$164	$886	$5	$47	$25	$0	$0	$0	$1,442
Air Force	O-9	Service chief staff headquarters	9	$341	$33	$783	$5	$31	$6	$0	$0	$0	$1,199
Air Force	O-9	Service component command	3	$323	$219	$487	$5	$40	$24	$0	$0	$0	$1,097
Air Force	O-9	Service secretariat	2	$341	$74	$581	$5	$87	$17	$0	$0	$0	$1,105
Air Force	O-10	All	9	$332	$460	$2,071	$5	$56	$47	$454	$291	$18	$3,733
Air Force	O-10	Major and service commands	6	$331	$441	$2,280	$5	$53	$45	$0	$0	$0	$3,154
Air Force	O-10	Service chief staff headquarters	2	$344	$565	$1,904	$5	$41	$21	$2,043	$543	$79	$5,545
Air Force	O-10	Service component command	1	$319	$364	$1,147	$5	$111	$111	$0	$1,530	$0	$3,586
Army	O-7	All	101	$289	$114	$181	$8	$39	$10	$0	$0	$1	$641
Army	O-7	Combatant command	1	$276	$0	$0	$8	b	b	$0	$0	$0	$283[c]
Army	O-7	Direct reporting and similar	39	$290	$113	$212	$8	$44	$12	$0	$0	$0	$678

Table A.4—Continued

Service	Grade	Organization Type	G/FO Count	G/FO Direct Cost	Staff Direct (Personal)[a]	Staff Direct (Positional)	G/FO Training	G/FO Travel	Staff Travel	G/FO MILAIR	G/FO PSD	G/FO Quarters	Total
Army	O-7	Major and service commands	12	$282	$163	$226	$8	$41	$0	$0	$0	$0	$719
Army	O-7	Operating forces	19	$284	$237	$164	$8	$46	$18	$0	$0	$0	$757
Army	O-7	Service chief staff headquarters	14	$297	$0	$151	$8	$27	$4	$0	$0	$6	$494
Army	O-7	Service component command	13	$287	$52	$114	$8	$29	$10	$0	$0	$0	$500
Army	O-7	Service secretariat	3	$300	$0	$190	$8	$13	$3	$0	$0	$0	$513
Army	O-8	All	82	$322	$203	$308	$8	$36	$20	$0	$0	$6	$903
Army	O-8	Direct reporting and similar	27	$324	$134	$409	$8	$39	$27	$0	$0	$7	$947
Army	O-8	Major and service commands	14	$315	$207	$487	$8	$37	$20	$0	$0	$0	$1,074
Army	O-8	Operating forces	17	$319	$452	$155	$8	$30	$4	$0	$0	$0	$967
Army	O-8	Service chief staff headquarters	9	$333	$0	$198	$8	$20	$15	$0	$0	$32	$605
Army	O-8	Service component command	9	$319	$235	$177	$8	$71	$51	$0	$0	$0	$861

Table A.4—Continued

Service	Grade	Organization Type	G/FO Count	G/FO Direct Cost	Staff Direct (Personal)[a]	Staff Direct (Positional)	G/FO Training	G/FO Travel	Staff Travel	G/FO MILAIR	G/FO PSD	G/FO Quarters	Total
Army	O-8	Service secretariat	6	$330	$56	$227	$8	$20	$2	$0	$0	$10	$655
Army	O-9	All	34	$342	$256	$624	$8	$34	$16	$0	$0	$33	$1,313
Army	O-9	Direct reporting and similar	5	$344	$303	$578	$8	$23	$18	$0	$0	$108	$1,382
Army	O-9	Major and service commands	6	$334	$261	$826	$8	$41	$33	$0	$0	$10	$1,514
Army	O-9	Operating forces	3	$334	$446	$124	$8	$15	$0	$0	$0	$0	$927
Army	O-9	Service chief staff headquarters	9	$350	$118	$738	$8	$25	$17	$0	$0	$56	$1,312
Army	O-9	Service component command	7	$334	$439	$473	$8	$66	$12	$0	$0	$0	$1,331
Army	O-9	Service secretariat	4	$350	$38	$765	$8	$15	$10	$0	$0	$0	$1,185
Army	O-10	All	7	$342	$483	$1,624	$8	$38	$66	$527	$565	$50	$3,703
Army	O-10	Major and service commands	3	$332	$302	$1,562	$8	$41	$68	$0	$0	$0	$2,314
Army	O-10	Service chief staff headquarters	2	$351	$615	$2,889	$8	$35	$130	$1,843	$1,979	$175	$8,024

Table A.4—Continued

Service	Grade	Organization Type	G/FO Count	G/FO Direct Cost	Staff Direct (Personal)[a]	Staff Direct (Positional)	G/FO Training	G/FO Travel	Staff Travel	G/FO MILAIR	G/FO PSD	G/FO Quarters	Total
Army	O-10	Service component command	2	$348	$623	$452	$8	$37	$0	$0	$0	$0	$1,466
Joint	O-7	All	110	$290	$14	$129	$5	$15	$1	$0	$0	$0	$454
Joint	O-7	Combatant command	47	$286	$4	$132	$5	$21	$1	$0	$0	$0	$449
Joint	O-7	Defense, joint, or service agency	22	$288	$28	$121	$5	$8	$0	$0	$0	$0	$450
Joint	O-7	Joint staff	24	$295	$8	$80	$5	$8	$0	$0	$0	$0	$397
Joint	O-7	National	2	$296	$0	$0	$5	b	b	$0	$0	$0	$302[c]
Joint	O-7	OSD	7	$294	$0	$248	$5	b	b	$0	$0	$0	$548[c]
Joint	O-7	Theater	8	$298	$67	$205	$5	b	b	$0	$0	$0	$577[c]
Joint	O-8	All	89	$322	$33	$220	$5	$29	$11	$0	$0	$5	$625
Joint	O-8	Combatant command	46	$318	$44	$258	$5	$33	$13	$0	$0	$1	$672
Joint	O-8	Defense, joint, or service agency	20	$324	$10	$142	$5	$39	$0	$0	$0	$0	$521
Joint	O-8	Joint staff	9	$328	$0	$169	$5	$13	$5	$0	$0	$24	$544
Joint	O-8	National	4	$327	$0	$0	$5	b	b	$0	$0	$0	$332[c]

Table A.4—Continued

Service	Grade	Organization Type	G/FO Count	G/FO Direct Cost	Staff Direct (Personal)[a]	Staff Direct (Positional)	G/FO Training	G/FO Travel	Staff Travel	G/FO MILAIR	G/FO PSD	G/FO Quarters	Total
Joint	O-8	OSD	2	$328	$0	$0	$5	b	b	$0	$0	$0	$333[c]
Joint	O-8	Other	1	$333	$152	$217	$5	$38	$0	$0	$0	$155	$901
Joint	O-8	Theater	7	$332	$78	$449	$5	b	b	$0	$0	$0	$865[c]
Joint	O-9	All	40	$338	$106	$269	$5	$22	$7	$0	$0	$13	$761
Joint	O-9	Combatant command	12	$331	$179	$296	$5	$26	$12	$0	$0	$9	$858
Joint	O-9	Defense, joint, or service agency	9	$338	$99	$230	$5	b	b	$0	$0	$0	$672[c]
Joint	O-9	Joint staff	7	$343	$66	$393	$5	$9	$1	$0	$0	$61	$880
Joint	O-9	National	6	$346	$50	$86	$5	b	b	$0	$0	$0	$489[c]
Joint	O-9	OSD	3	$337	$0	$91	$5	b	b	$0	$0	$0	$433[c]
Joint	O-9	Operating forces	2	$325	$232	$794	$5	$48	$0	$0	$0	$0	$1,404
Joint	O-9	Theater	1	$350	$0	$0	$5	b	b	$0	$0	$0	$355[c]
Joint	O-10	All	15	$336	$594	$2,194	$5	$47	$340	$5,366	$1,909	$29	$10,818
Joint	O-10	Combatant command	11	$333	$580	$2,269	$5	$38	$210	$5,693	$1,736	$11	$10,875
Joint	O-10	Joint staff	2	$338	$676	$3,370	$5	$87	$922	$4,971	$4,104	$158	$14,632

Table A.4—Continued

Service	Grade	Organization Type	G/FO Count	G/FO Direct Cost	Staff Direct (Personal)[a]	Staff Direct (Positional)	G/FO Training	G/FO Travel	Staff Travel	G/FO MILAIR	G/FO PSD	G/FO Quarters	Total
Joint	O-10	National	1	$342	$518	$809	$5	b	b	$3,185	$1,326	$0	$6,176[c]
Joint	O-10	Theater	1	$349	$659	$399	$5	b	b	$4,750	$0	$0	$6,161[c]
Marines	O-7	All	22	$283	$184	$361	$5	$22[d]	$3[d]	$0	$0	$3	$860[c]
Marines	O-7	Direct reporting and similar	8	$282	$256	$452	$5	$12[d]	$1[d]	$0	$0	$2	$1,009[c]
Marines	O-7	Operating forces	4	$275	$294	$207	$5	$90[d]	$4[d]	$0	$0	$0	$875[c]
Marines	O-7	Service chief staff headquarters	8	$284	$38	$427	$5	$10[d]	$3[d]	$0	$0	$0	$767[c]
Marines	O-7	Service component command	2	$296	$258	$45	$5	$34[d]	$7[d]	$0	$0	$23	$669[c]
Marines	O-8	All	22	$309	$224	$229	$5	$61[d]	$6[d]	$0	$0	$3	$837[c]
Marines	O-8	Direct reporting and similar	2	$301	$414	$271	$5	$80[d]	$4[d]	$0	$0	$0	$1,074[c]
Marines	O-8	Major and service commands	2	$304	$240	$50	$5	$39[d]	$17[d]	$0	$0	$0	$654[c]
Marines	O-8	Operating forces	9	$308	$269	$242	$5	$62[d]	$4[d]	$0	$0	$8	$898[c]
Marines	O-8	Service chief staff headquarters	5	$317	$58	$224	$5	$75[d]	$5[d]	$0	$0	$0	$685[c]

Table A.4—Continued

Service	Grade	Organization Type	G/FO Count	G/FO Direct Cost	Staff Direct (Personal)[a]	Staff Direct (Positional)	G/FO Training	G/FO Travel	Staff Travel	G/FO MILAIR	G/FO PSD	G/FO Quarters	Total
Marines	O-8	Service component command	4	$308	$229	$275	$5	$45[d]	$6[d]	$0	$0	$0	$868[c]
Marines	O-9	All	15	$327	$355	$696	$5	$66[d]	$4[d]	$0	$0	$5	$1,458[c]
Marines	O-9	Major and service commands	2	$323	$441	$398	$5	$6[d]	$1[d]	$0	$0	$12	$1,186[c]
Marines	O-9	Operating forces	3	$320	$437	$431	$5	$120[d]	$7[d]	$0	$0	$0	$1,320[c]
Marines	O-9	Service chief staff headquarters	7	$330	$192	$930	$5	$5[d]	$1[d]	$0	$0	$4	$1,466[c]
Marines	O-9	Service component command	3	$329	$599	$612	$5	$93[d]	$6[d]	$0	$0	$8	$1,653[c]
Marines	O-10	All	2	$337	$752	$2,902	$5	b	b	$1,943	$619	$91	$6,649[c]
Marines	O-10	Service chief staff headquarters	2	$337	$752	$2,902	$5	b	b	$1,943	$619	$91	$6,649[c]
Navy	O-7	All	74	$285	$92	$341[e]	$3	$38	$15[e]	$0	$0	$2	$775[c]
Navy	O-7	Defense, joint, or service agency	1	$285	$0	$567[e]	$3	b	b, e	$0	$0	$0	$856[c]
Navy	O-7	Direct reporting and similar	39	$286	$110	$313[e]	$3	$49	$18[e]	$0	$0	$2	$781[c]

Table A.4—Continued

Service	Grade	Organization Type	G/FO Count	G/FO Direct Cost	Staff Direct (Personal)[a]	Staff Direct (Positional)	G/FO Training	G/FO Travel	Staff Travel	G/FO MILAIR	G/FO PSD	G/FO Quarters	Total
Navy	O-7	Major and service commands	2	$283	$170	$721[e]	$3	$58	$53[e]	$0	$0	$0	$1,290[c]
Navy	O-7	Operating forces	18	$277	$86	$393[e]	$3	$23	$14[e]	$0	$0	$2	$799[c]
Navy	O-7	Service chief staff headquarters	8	$291	$51	$279[e]	$3	$9	$3[e]	$0	$0	$1	$638[c]
Navy	O-7	Service component command	4	$291	$0	$244[e]	$3	$38	$0[e]	$0	$0	$4	$581[c]
Navy	O-7	Service secretariat	2	$291	$98	$358[e]	$3	$77	$1[e]	$0	$0	$0	$822[c]
Navy	O-8	All	42	$320	$90	$572[e]	$3	$24	$14[e]	$0	$0	$11	$1,033[c]
Navy	O-8	Defense, joint, or service agency	1	$309	$0	$157[e]	$3	b	b, e	$0	$0	$0	$469[c]
Navy	O-8	Direct reporting and similar	15	$320	$123	$435[e]	$3	$30	$16[e]	$0	$0	$14	$941[c]
Navy	O-8	Major and service commands	4	$317	$246	$879[e]	$3	$20	$6[e]	$0	$0	$35	$1,508[c]
Navy	O-8	Operating forces	5	$313	$0	$470[e]	$3	$14	$10[e]	$0	$0	$7	$818[c]

Table A.4—Continued

Service	Grade	Organization Type	G/FO Count	G/FO Direct Cost	Staff Direct (Personal)[a]	Staff Direct (Positional)	G/FO Training	G/FO Travel	Staff Travel	G/FO MILAIR	G/FO PSD	G/FO Quarters	Total
Navy	O-8	Service chief staff headquarters	11	$323	$0	$633[e]	$3	$11	$2[e]	$0	$0	$5	$978[c]
Navy	O-8	Service component command	4	$321	$129	$848[e]	$3	$40	$40[e]	$0	$0	$4	$1,386[c]
Navy	O-8	Service secretariat	2	$323	$206	$568[e]	$3	$20	$17[e]	$0	$0	$0	$1,137[c]
Navy	O-9	All	27	$333	$233	$931[e]	$3	$28	$26[e]	$0	$84	$41	$1,678[c]
Navy	O-9	Direct reporting and similar	5	$335	$318	$665[e]	$3	$27	$19[e]	$0	$0	$67	$1,433[c]
Navy	O-9	Major and service commands	8	$330	$265	$1,197[e]	$3	$25	$42[e]	$0	$0	$33	$1,895[c]
Navy	O-9	Service chief staff headquarters	8	$336	$176	$988[e]	$3	$27	$23[e]	$0	$0	$28	$1,582[c]
Navy	O-9	Service component command	3	$326	$229	$674[e]	$3	$22	$18[e]	$0	$753	$76	$2,101[c]
Navy	O-9	Service secretariat	3	$336	$164	$769[e]	$3	$44	$16[e]	$0	$0	$18	$1,351[c]
Navy	O-10	All	6	$335	$642	$2,009[e]	$3	$33	$123[e]	$648	$166	$101	$4,061[c]
Navy	O-10	Other	1	$336	$509	$1,415[e]	$3	$22	$81[e]	$0	$0	$74	$2,441[c]

Table A.4—Continued

Service	Grade	Organization Type	G/FO Count	G/FO Direct Cost	Staff Direct (Personal)[a]	Staff Direct (Positional)	G/FO Training	G/FO Travel	Staff Travel	G/FO MILAIR	G/FO PSD	G/FO Quarters	Total
Navy	O-10	Service chief staff headquarters	2	$338	$862	$3,039[e]	$3	$54	$280[e]	$1,943[e]	$416	$107	$7,042[c]
Navy	O-10	Service component command	3	$333	$540	$1,521[e]	$3	$22	$33[e]	$0	$56	$105	$2,614[c]

NOTES: Reflects average total cost estimates of specific G/FO positions. Total cost estimates are based on our application of the cost-estimating framework discussed in Chapter Two to the positions identified from manning documents provided for this study. Estimated values in 2018 dollars. G/FO positions are categorized based on Harrington et al. (2018). "Direct Reporting and Similar" includes direct reporting units, shore-based bureaus, acquisition activities, supporting establishments, and field operating agencies.

[a] Direct costs of security personnel for G/FOs requiring continuous support are associated with the column "General or Flag Officer Security."

[b] Missing data from DTMO.

[c] Totals are missing some cost categories and would increase if more data became available.

[d] We are not currently able to link all Marine Corps service member travel costs to Marine Corps G/FOs.

[e] Manning documents for the Navy exclude civilians.

Table A.5
Average Annual Total Costs (in Thousands) by Service, Grade, and Functional Category

Service	Grade	Functional Category	G/FO Count	G/FO Direct Cost	Staff Direct (Personal)[a]	Staff Direct (Positional)	G/FO Training	G/FO Travel	Staff Travel	G/FO MILAIR	G/FO PSD	G/FO Quarters	Total
Air Force	O-7	All	94	$282	$20	$335	$5	$30	$2	$0	$0	$0	$673
Air Force	O-7	Acquisition/R&D	14	$286	$42	$392	$5	$30	$7	$0	$0	$0	$762
Air Force	O-7	C4I	2	$293	$0	$340	$5	$28	$0	$0	$0	$0	$666
Air Force	O-7	Engineer	1	$293	$0	$377	$5	$5	$0	$0	$0	$0	$680
Air Force	O-7	FMET	5	$283	$27	$604	$5	$22	$1	$0	$0	$0	$942
Air Force	O-7	Intelligence	4	$289	$0	$272	$5	$16	$0	$0	$0	$0	$582
Air Force	O-7	Manpower	2	$286	$0	$516	$5	$21	$1	$0	$0	$0	$827
Air Force	O-7	Materiel and logistics	11	$279	$36	$260	$5	$30	$0	$0	$0	$0	$609
Air Force	O-7	Military operations	26	$277	$23	$322	$5	$38	$1	$0	$0	$0	$665
Air Force	O-7	Other	4	$281	$34	$735	$5	$29	$0	$0	$0	$0	$1,084
Air Force	O-7	Program and financial management	4	$281	$0	$157	$5	$13	$0	$0	$0	$0	$456
Air Force	O-7	Special staff	12	$286	$0	$284	$5	$27	$1	$0	$0	$0	$602
Air Force	O-7	Strategic plans and policy	9	$285	$0	$181	$5	$31	$0	$0	$0	$0	$502
Air Force	O-8	All	49	$321	$67	$589	$5	$29	$6	$0	$0	$0	$1,018
Air Force	O-8	Acquisition/R&D	4	$319	$0	$328	$5	$18	$6	$0	$0	$0	$676

Table A.5—Continued

Service	Grade	Functional Category	G/FO Count	G/FO Direct Cost	Staff Direct (Personal)[a]	Staff Direct (Positional)	G/FO Training	G/FO Travel	Staff Travel	G/FO MILAIR	G/FO PSD	G/FO Quarters	Total
Air Force	O-8	FMET	2	$312	$69	$1,068	$5	$17	$0	$0	$0	$0	$1,470
Air Force	O-8	Intelligence	1	$328	$0	$0	$5	$17	$0	$0	$0	$0	$350
Air Force	O-8	Manpower	2	$321	$0	$674	$5	$4	$1	$0	$0	$0	$1,004
Air Force	O-8	Materiel and logistics	4	$316	$77	$604	$5	$24	$7	$0	$0	$0	$1,033
Air Force	O-8	Military operations	17	$317	$131	$634	$5	$47	$11	$0	$0	$0	$1,145
Air Force	O-8	Other	5	$325	$125	$1,009	$5	$10	$4	$0	$0	$0	$1,478
Air Force	O-8	Program and financial management	4	$328	$0	$366	$5	$11	$0	$0	$0	$0	$711
Air Force	O-8	Special staff	8	$328	$0	$528	$5	$35	$5	$0	$0	$0	$900
Air Force	O-8	Strategic plans and policy	2	$313	$0	$81	$5	$10	$0	$0	$0	$0	$408
Air Force	O-9	All	28	$333	$140	$904	$5	$42	$12	$0	$0	$3	$1,439
Air Force	O-9	Acquisition/ R&D	3	$339	$202	$1,363	$5	$36	$6	$0	$0	$0	$1,950
Air Force	O-9	FMET	4	$329	$272	$794	$5	$45	$7	$0	$0	$23	$1,475
Air Force	O-9	Intelligence	1	$341	$0	$0	$5	$24	$18	$0	$0	$0	$388
Air Force	O-9	Manpower	1	$341	$0	$1,709	$5	$1	$0	$0	$0	$0	$2,056
Air Force	O-9	Materiel and logistics	2	$332	$226	$1,332	$5	$32	$24	$0	$0	$0	$1,951

Table A.5—Continued

Service	Grade	Functional Category	G/FO Count	G/FO Direct Cost	Staff Direct (Personal)[a]	Staff Direct (Positional)	G/FO Training	G/FO Travel	Staff Travel	G/FO MILAIR	G/FO PSD	G/FO Quarters	Total
Air Force	O-9	Military operations	7	$325	$183	$739	$5	$47	$18	$0	$0	$0	$1,317
Air Force	O-9	Other	5	$330	$99	$926	$5	$48	$0	$0	$0	$0	$1,408
Air Force	O-9	Special staff	3	$341	$0	$617	$5	$64	$21	$0	$0	$0	$1,048
Air Force	O-9	Strategic plans and policy	2	$341	$0	$1,007	$5	$32	$2	$0	$0	$0	$1,387
Air Force	O-10	All	9	$332	$460	$2,071	$5	$56	$47	$454	$291	$18	$3,733
Air Force	O-10	Military operations	1	$319	$364	$1,147	$5	$111	$111	$0	$1,530	$0	$3,586
Air Force	O-10	Other	8	$334	$472	$2,186	$5	$50	$39	$511	$136	$20	$3,752
Army	O-7	All	101	$289	$114	$181	$8	$39	$10	$0	$0	$1	$641
Army	O-7	Acquisition/R&D	14	$289	$81	$187	$8	$27	$20	$0	$0	$0	$612
Army	O-7	C4I	1	$281	$0	$160	$8	$61	$1	$0	$0	$0	$512
Army	O-7	CD&I	5	$290	$31	$151	$8	$32	$10	$0	$0	$0	$521
Army	O-7	Engineer	4	$296	$0	$0	$8	$32	$0	$0	$0	$0	$336
Army	O-7	FMET	24	$286	$191	$350	$8	$49	$5	$0	$0	$0	$889
Army	O-7	Manpower	3	$281	$0	$155	$8	$78	$13	$0	$0	$0	$536
Army	O-7	Materiel and logistics	6	$285	$236	$137	$8	$21	$13	$0	$0	$0	$700
Army	O-7	Military operations	21	$286	$158	$71	$8	$41	$16	$0	$0	$4	$585

Table A.5—Continued

Service	Grade	Functional Category	G/FO Count	G/FO Direct Cost	Staff Direct (Personal)[a]	Staff Direct (Positional)	G/FO Training	G/FO Travel	Staff Travel	G/FO MILAIR	G/FO PSD	G/FO Quarters	Total
Army	O-7	Other	3	$292	$0	$97	$8	$40	$0	$0	$0	$0	$436
Army	O-7	Program and financial management	2	$300	$0	$50	$8	$8	$0	$0	$0	$0	$365
Army	O-7	Special staff	16	$292	$56	$186	$8	$33	$8	$0	$0	$0	$582
Army	O-7	Strategic plans and policy	2	$300	$0	$111	$8	$1	$1	$0	$0	$0	$421
Army	O-8	All	82	$322	$203	$308	$8	$36	$20	$0	$0	$6	$903
Army	O-8	Acquisition/R&D	9	$326	$100	$404	$8	$35	$47	$0	$0	$0	$920
Army	O-8	C4I	2	$329	$97	$472	$8	$36	$24	$0	$0	$0	$965
Army	O-8	Engineer	6	$332	$37	$134	$8	$1	$0	$0	$0	$3	$515
Army	O-8	FMET	15	$317	$235	$560	$8	$38	$5	$0	$0	$0	$1,162
Army	O-8	Manpower	3	$321	$101	$561	$8	$49	$13	$0	$0	$0	$1,054
Army	O-8	Materiel and logistics	11	$322	$150	$359	$8	$55	$63	$0	$0	$0	$956
Army	O-8	Military operations	23	$319	$414	$179	$8	$34	$9	$0	$0	$15	$979
Army	O-8	Other	1	$318	$0	$90	$8	$110	$146	$0	$0	$0	$671
Army	O-8	Program and financial management	4	$324	$47	$112	$8	$27	$0	$0	$0	$0	$518
Army	O-8	Special staff	7	$330	$22	$163	$8	$27	$7	$0	$0	$25	$580

Table A.5—Continued

Service	Grade	Functional Category	G/FO Count	G/FO Direct Cost	Staff Direct (Personal)[a]	Staff Direct (Positional)	G/FO Training	G/FO Travel	Staff Travel	G/FO MILAIR	G/FO PSD	G/FO Quarters	Total
Army	O-8	Strategic plans and policy	1	$333	$0	$0	$8	b	b	$0	$0	$0	$341[c]
Army	O-9	All	34	$342	$256	$624	$8	$34	$16	$0	$0	$33	$1,313
Army	O-9	Acquisition/ R&D	1	$350	$0	$1,180	$8	$21	$7	$0	$0	$0	$1,565
Army	O-9	C4I	1	$350	$152	$773	$8	$22	$3	$0	$0	$0	$1,307
Army	O-9	CD&I	1	$334	$333	$289	$8	$23	$3	$0	$0	$0	$989
Army	O-9	Engineer	1	$350	$152	$0	$8	$1	$0	$0	$0	$118	$629
Army	O-9	FMET	4	$340	$341	$1,283	$8	$39	$43	$0	$0	$15	$2,069
Army	O-9	Intelligence	1	$350	$0	$1,588	$8	$12	$1	$0	$0	$0	$1,958
Army	O-9	Manpower	1	$350	$152	$803	$8	$11	$9	$0	$0	$0	$1,332
Army	O-9	Materiel and logistics	4	$342	$198	$531	$8	$36	$48	$0	$0	$79	$1,244
Army	O-9	Military operations	11	$335	$394	$391	$8	$52	$10	$0	$0	$14	$1,203
Army	O-9	Other	3	$345	$252	$817	$8	$23	$0	$0	$0	$25	$1,470
Army	O-9	Program and financial management	2	$350	$76	$837	$8	$14	$17	$0	$0	$32	$1,333
Army	O-9	Special Staff	3	$350	$51	$132	$8	$30	$3	$0	$0	$105	$679
Army	O-9	Strategic plans and policy	1	$339	$368	$511	$8	$5	$0	$0	$0	$0	$1,230

Table A.5—Continued

Service	Grade	Functional Category	G/FO Count	G/FO Direct Cost	Staff Direct (Personal)[a]	Staff Direct (Positional)	G/FO Training	G/FO Travel	Staff Travel	G/FO MILAIR	G/FO PSD	G/FO Quarters	Total
Army	O-10	All	7	$342	$483	$1,624	$8	$38	$66	$527	$565	$50	$3,703
Army	O-10	FMET	1	$334	$139	$1,076	$8	$4	$12	$0	$0	$0	$1,572
Army	O-10	Materiel and logistics	1	$333	$632	$2,377	$8	$83	$138	$0	$0	$0	$3,572
Army	O-10	Military operations	2	$344	$429	$694	$8	$52	$27	$0	$0	$0	$1,554
Army	O-10	Other	2	$351	$615	$2,889	$8	$35	$130	$1,843	$1,979	$175	$8,024
Army	O-10	Strategic plans and policy	1	$338	$523	$747	$8	$5	$0	$0	$0	$0	$1,621
Joint	O-7	All	110	$290	$14	$129	$5	$15	$1	$0	$0	$0	$454
Joint	O-7	Acquisition/ R&D	4	$294	$0	$185	$5	$2	$0	$0	$0	$0	$486
Joint	O-7	C4I	5	$287	$0	$134	$5	$11	$1	$0	$0	$0	$438
Joint	O-7	CD&I	4	$288	$0	$20	$5	$11	$1	$0	$0	$0	$325
Joint	O-7	FMET	6	$294	$31	$73	$5	$1	$0	$0	$0	$0	$403
Joint	O-7	Intelligence	19	$284	$8	$156	$5	$26	$2	$0	$0	$0	$482
Joint	O-7	Manpower	3	$298	$86	$212	$5	$27	$0	$0	$0	$0	$627
Joint	O-7	Materiel and logistics	10	$286	$20	$110	$5	$19	$1	$0	$0	$0	$441
Joint	O-7	Military operations	33	$292	$22	$90	$5	$12	[b]	$0	$0	$0	$422
Joint	O-7	Other	3	$289	$0	$413	$5	[b]	[b]	$0	$0	$0	$707[c]

Table A.5—Continued

Service	Grade	Functional Category	G/FO Count	G/FO Direct Cost	Staff Direct (Personal)[a]	Staff Direct (Positional)	G/FO Training	G/FO Travel	Staff Travel	G/FO MILAIR	G/FO PSD	G/FO Quarters	Total
Joint	O-7	Program and financial management	1	$294	$0	$95	$5	$6	$0	$0	$0	$0	$400
Joint	O-7	Special staff	3	$295	$0	$397	$5	$3	$0	$0	$0	$0	$699
Joint	O-7	Strategic plans and policy	19	$292	$0	$108	$5	$16	$0	$0	$0	$0	$422
Joint	O-8	All	89	$322	$33	$220	$5	$29	$11	$0	$0	$5	$625
Joint	O-8	Acquisition/R&D	7	$325	$28	$52	$5	$18	$16	$0	$0	$0	$443
Joint	O-8	C4I	3	$321	$0	$179	$5	$19	$0	$0	$0	$0	$524
Joint	O-8	CD&I	4	$327	$0	$104	$5	$20	$0	$0	$0	$0	$457
Joint	O-8	FMET	3	$331	$51	$204	$5	$27	$0	$0	$0	$52	$669
Joint	O-8	Intelligence	12	$325	$12	$156	$5	$21	$0	$0	$0	$0	$519
Joint	O-8	Manpower	3	$320	$0	$286	$5	$17	$0	$0	$0	$0	$628
Joint	O-8	Materiel and logistics	6	$326	$0	$521	$5	$36	$23	$0	$0	$0	$910
Joint	O-8	Military operations	25	$321	$90	$277	$5	$49	$18	$0	$0	$1	$761
Joint	O-8	Other	8	$320	$0	$316	$5	$17	$12	$0	$0	$22	$694
Joint	O-8	Program and financial management	1	$313	$0	$0	$5	b	b	$0	$0	$0	$318c
Joint	O-8	Special staff	3	$328	$0	$0	$5	$18	$16	$0	$0	$0	$367

Table A.5—Continued

Service	Grade	Functional Category	G/FO Count	G/FO Direct Cost	Staff Direct (Personal)[a]	Staff Direct (Positional)	G/FO Training	G/FO Travel	Staff Travel	G/FO MILAIR	G/FO PSD	G/FO Quarters	Total
Joint	O-8	Strategic plans and policy	14	$317	$12	$170	$5	$22	$7	$0	$0	$5	$539
Joint	O-9	All	40	$338	$106	$269	$5	$22	$7	$0	$0	$13	$761
Joint	O-9	Acquisition/R&D	4	$341	$38	$199	$5	$1	$0	$0	$0	$31	$614
Joint	O-9	C4I	2	$339	$0	$511	$5	$3	$0	$0	$0	$0	$857
Joint	O-9	FMET	3	$335	$222	$350	$5	$16	$0	$0	$0	$0	$932
Joint	O-9	Intelligence	3	$347	$51	$0	$5	b	b	$0	$0	$0	$403[c]
Joint	O-9	Manpower	1	$335	$0	$0	$5	b	b	$0	$0	$0	$340[c]
Joint	O-9	Materiel and logistics	3	$337	$116	$371	$5	$5	$0	$0	$0	$21	$857
Joint	O-9	Military operations	16	$333	$146	$321	$5	$26	$11	$0	$0	$11	$853
Joint	O-9	Other	3	$340	$47	$118	$5	$89	$0	$0	$0	$0	$598
Joint	O-9	Special staff	1	$336	$0	$159	$5	b	b	$0	$0	$0	$500[c]
Joint	O-9	Strategic plans and policy	4	$348	$113	$283	$5	$8	$4	$0	$0	$43	$806
Joint	O-10	All	15	$336	$594	$2,194	$5	$47	$340	$5,366	$1,909	$29	$10,818
Joint	O-10	FMET	1	$342	$518	$809	$5	b	b	$3,185	$1,326	$0	$6,176[c]
Joint	O-10	Materiel and logistics	1	$334	$596	$1,645	$5	$19	$21	$2,548	$644	$0	$5,812

Table A.5—Continued

Service	Grade	Functional Category	G/FO Count	G/FO Direct Cost	Staff Direct (Personal)[a]	Staff Direct (Positional)	G/FO Training	G/FO Travel	Staff Travel	G/FO MILAIR	G/FO PSD	G/FO Quarters	Total
Joint	O-10	Military operations	11	$335	$585	$2,156	$5	$40	$234	$5,893	$1,678	$11	$10,936
Joint	O-10	Other	2	$338	$676	$3,370	$5	$87	$922	$4,971	$4,104	$158	$14,632
Marines	O-7	All	22	$283	$184	$361	$5	$22[d]	$3[d]	$0	$0	$3	$860[c]
Marines	O-7	Acquisition/R&D	1	$264	$307	$480	$5	$4[d]	$0[d]	$0	$0	$0	$1,060[c]
Marines	O-7	C4I	1	$290	$0	$1,053	$5	$1[d]	$0[d]	$0	$0	$0	$1,349[c]
Marines	O-7	CD&I	1	$282	$0	$364	$5	$18[d]	$2[d]	$0	$0	$0	$671[c]
Marines	O-7	FMET	4	$282	$185	$449	$5	$14[d]	$1[d]	$0	$0	$0	$936[c]
Marines	O-7	Manpower	1	$279	$314	$457	$5	$9[d]	$2[d]	$0	$0	$14	$1,079[c]
Marines	O-7	Materiel and logistics	6	$276	$333	$304	$5	$24[d]	$6[d]	$0	$0	$0	$948[c]
Marines	O-7	Military operations	4	$289	$171	$118	$5	$57[d]	$5[d]	$0	$0	$12	$657[c]
Marines	O-7	Special staff	3	$290	$0	$373	$5	$1[d]	$0[d]	$0	$0	$0	$669[c]
Marines	O-7	Strategic plans and policy	1	$290	$0	$383	$5	$1[d]	$0[d]	$0	$0	$0	$679[c]
Marines	O-8	All	22	$309	$224	$229	$5	$61[d]	$6[d]	$0	$0	$3	$837[c]
Marines	O-8	C4I	1	$316	$188	$373	$5	[b]	[b]	$0	$0	$0	$883[c]
Marines	O-8	CD&I	1	$313	$0	$100	$5	$10[d]	$0[d]	$0	$0	$0	$429[c]
Marines	O-8	FMET	1	$313	$294	$100	$5	$39[d]	$17[d]	$0	$0	$0	$769[c]

Table A.5—Continued

Service	Grade	Functional Category	G/FO Count	G/FO Direct Cost	Staff Direct (Personal)[a]	Staff Direct (Positional)	G/FO Training	G/FO Travel	Staff Travel	G/FO MILAIR	G/FO PSD	G/FO Quarters	Total
Marines	O-8	Manpower	2	$313	$145	$351	$5	$140[d]	$11[d]	$0	$0	$0	$964[c]
Marines	O-8	Materiel and logistics	2	$301	$414	$271	$5	$80[d]	$4[d]	$0	$0	$0	$1,074[c]
Marines	O-8	Military operations	13	$306	$257	$224	$5	$57[d]	$5[d]	$0	$0	$5	$858[c]
Marines	O-8	Program and financial management	1	$322	$0	$0	$5	b	b	$0	$0	$0	$327[c]
Marines	O-8	Special staff	1	$322	$0	$321	$5	b	b	$0	$0	$0	$648[c]
Marines	O-9	All	15	$327	$355	$696	$5	$66[d]	$4[d]	$0	$0	$5	$1,458[c]
Marines	O-9	CD&I	1	$326	$243	$418	$5	$9[d]	$2[d]	$0	$0	$6	$1,009[c]
Marines	O-9	Manpower	1	$326	$0	$910	$5	$9[d]	$2[d]	$0	$0	$0	$1,251[c]
Marines	O-9	Materiel and logistics	1	$310	$346	$693	$5	$2[d]	$0[d]	$0	$0	$0	$1,356[c]
Marines	O-9	Military operations	10	$327	$432	$742	$5	$92[d]	$6[d]	$0	$0	$7	$1,610[c]
Marines	O-9	Program and financial management	1	$335	$213	$523	$5	b	b	$0	$0	$0	$1,075[c]
Marines	O-9	Special staff	1	$335	$213	$469	$5	b	b	$0	$0	$0	$1,021[c]
Marines	O-10	All	2	$337	$752	$2,902	$5	b	b	$1,943	$619	$91	$6,649[c]
Marines	O-10	Military operations	2	$337	$752	$2,902	$5	b	b	$1,943	$619	$91	$6,649[c]

Table A.5—Continued

Service	Grade	Functional Category	G/FO Count	G/FO Direct Cost	Staff Direct (Personal)[a]	Staff Direct (Positional)	G/FO Training	G/FO Travel	Staff Travel	G/FO MILAIR	G/FO PSD	G/FO Quarters	Total
Navy	O-7	All	74	$285	$92	$341[e]	$3	$38	$15[e]	$0	$0	$2	$775[c]
Navy	O-7	Acquisition/R&D	10	$288	$0	$129[e]	$3	$52	$5[e]	$0	$0	$0	$476[c]
Navy	O-7	C4I	1	$296	$0	$85[e]	$3	$82	$2[e]	$0	$0	$2	$470[c]
Navy	O-7	CD&I	4	$286	$142	$361[e]	$3	$48	$25[e]	$0	$0	$1	$866[c]
Navy	O-7	Engineer	3	$292	$129	$279[e]	$3	$55	$33[e]	$0	$0	$0	$790[c]
Navy	O-7	FMET	2	$284	$257	$329[e]	$3	$41	$17[e]	$0	$0	$0	$932[c]
Navy	O-7	Intelligence	1	$285	$0	$567[e]	$3	b	b, e	$0	$0	$0	$856[c]
Navy	O-7	Manpower	4	$278	$78	$353[e]	$3	$29	$17[e]	$0	$0	$0	$757[c]
Navy	O-7	Materiel and logistics	15	$288	$169	$311[e]	$3	$26	$11[e]	$0	$0	$5	$813[c]
Navy	O-7	Military operations	25	$279	$76	$413[e]	$3	$30	$15[e]	$0	$0	$1	$817[c]
Navy	O-7	Special staff	7	$289	$87	$460[e]	$3	$68	$29[e]	$0	$0	$0	$936[c]
Navy	O-7	Strategic plans and policy	2	$306	$0	$346[e]	$3	$55	$0[e]	$0	$0	$9	$720[c]
Navy	O-8	All	42	$320	$90	$572[e]	$3	$24	$14[e]	$0	$0	$11	$1,033[c]
Navy	O-8	Acquisition/R&D	7	$322	$59	$354[e]	$3	$42	$20[e]	$0	$0	$10	$810[c]
Navy	O-8	C4I	1	$323	$0	$433[e]	$3	b	b, e	$0	$0	$0	$759[c]
Navy	O-8	CD&I	4	$321	$46	$738[e]	$3	$4	$1[e]	$0	$0	$1	$1,115[c]

Table A.5—Continued

Service	Grade	Functional Category	G/FO Count	G/FO Direct Cost	Staff Direct (Personal)[a]	Staff Direct (Positional)	G/FO Training	G/FO Travel	Staff Travel	G/FO MILAIR	G/FO PSD	G/FO Quarters	Total
Navy	O-8	Engineer	1	$323	$196	$157[e]	$3	$3	$2[e]	$0	$0	$0	$684[c]
Navy	O-8	FMET	3	$314	$323	$732[e]	$3	$39	$25[e]	$0	$0	$30	$1,466[c]
Navy	O-8	Intelligence	1	$329	$0	$157[e]	$3	$1	$0[e]	$0	$0	$0	$491[c]
Navy	O-8	Manpower	1	$323	$0	$1,090[e]	$3	$20	$8[e]	$0	$0	$0	$1,444[c]
Navy	O-8	Materiel and logistics	3	$314	$51	$370[e]	$3	$25	$22[e]	$0	$0	$6	$792[c]
Navy	O-8	Military operations	15	$318	$79	$651[e]	$3	$24	$18[e]	$0	$0	$13	$1,107[c]
Navy	O-8	Program and financial management	2	$323	$0	$683[e]	$3	$2	$0[e]	$0	$0	$20	$1,032[c]
Navy	O-8	Special staff	4	$323	$163	$584[e]	$3	$18	$4[e]	$0	$0	$8	$1,103[c]
Navy	O-9	All	27	$333	$233	$931[e]	$3	$28	$26[e]	$0	$84	$41	$1,678[c]
Navy	O-9	Acquisition/R&D	3	$333	$207	$773[e]	$3	$16	$6[e]	$0	$0	$13	$1,350[c]
Navy	O-9	C4I	2	$333	$169	$751[e]	$3	$28	$10[e]	$0	$0	$0	$1,293[c]
Navy	O-9	CD&I	1	$336	$216	$1,617[e]	$3	$22	$18[e]	$0	$0	$0	$2,211[c]
Navy	O-9	FMET	1	$338	$665	$1,026[e]	$3	$37	$38[e]	$0	$0	$299	$2,406[c]
Navy	O-9	Manpower	2	$336	$147	$367[e]	$3	$22	$18[e]	$0	$0	$14	$905[c]
Navy	O-9	Materiel and logistics	3	$336	$379	$904[e]	$3	$41	$36[e]	$0	$0	$51	$1,750[c]

Table A.5—Continued

Service	Grade	Functional Category	G/FO Count	G/FO Direct Cost	Staff Direct (Personal)[a]	Staff Direct (Positional)	G/FO Training	G/FO Travel	Staff Travel	G/FO MILAIR	G/FO PSD	G/FO Quarters	Total
Navy	O-9	Military operations	11	$329	$256	$1,117[e]	$3	$22	$36[e]	$0	$205	$50	$2,019[c]
Navy	O-9	Program and financial management	1	$336	$0	$1,050[e]	$3	$22	$18[e]	$0	$0	$0	$1,428[c]
Navy	O-9	Special staff	3	$336	$72	$628[e]	$3	$48	$21[e]	$0	$0	$15	$1,124[c]
Navy	O-10	All	6	$335	$642	$2,009[e]	$3	$33	$123[e]	$648	$166	$101	$4,061[c]
Navy	O-10	Military operations	3	$333	$540	$1,521[e]	$3	$22	$33[e]	$0	$56	$105	$2,614[c]
Navy	O-10	Other	3	$337	$744	$2,498[e]	$3	$43	$214[e]	$1,295	$277	$96	$5,508[c]

NOTES: Reflects average total cost estimates of specific G/FO positions. Total cost estimates are based on our application of the cost-estimating framework discussed in Chapter Two to the positions identified from manning documents provided for this study. Estimated values in 2018 dollars. G/FO positions are categorized based on Harrington et al. (2018). Special staff include legal, medical, public affairs, chaplain, and congressional affairs; and power includes personnel functions.

[a] Direct costs of security personnel for G/FOs requiring continuous support are associated with the column "General or Flag Officer Security."

[b] Missing data from DTMO.

[c] These totals are missing some cost categories and would increase if more data became available.

[d] We are not currently able to link all Marine Corps service member travel costs to Marine Corps G/FOs.

[e] Manning documents for the Navy exclude civilians.

APPENDIX B

Categorization and Association of Support Positions

In this appendix, we provide detail about our textual categorization of positions into GO or FO personal and positional support positions as discussed in Chapter Two. Additionally, we provide detail about how we associate support positions with specific G/FO positions. We discuss each of the service and joint duty organizations in separate sections. In an effort to make our decision rules consistent across the services, we use similar terminology to categorize positions where possible. Therefore, not all decision rules may be applicable to each service or joint duty assignments.

B.1. Air Force GO Support Positions

We derived the Air Force sample from manning documents of units with at least one GO assigned in FY 2018 (units are identified by UIC). For the Air Force, manning documents reflect tables of organization extracted from the Air Force's Manpower Programming and Execution System. These data were provided by the Office of the Deputy Chief of Staff of the Air Force for Personnel (AF/A1).

Identify Personal Staff for Air Force GOs
- Aides-de-camp: any position satisfying one of the following conditions:
  - any Air Force Specialty Code (AFSC) title with "AIDE DE CAMP", "AIDE-DE-CAMP", or "AIDE TO" as part of it
  - any AFSC or duty title exactly equal to "AIDE".
- Enlisted aides: identified by a separate file provided by OSD General Officer Management Office (GOMO).
- Drivers: any position satisfying one of the following conditions:
  - any AFSC title exactly equal to "ADMIN ASST / DRIVER" or "ENLISTED ASST/DRIVER".

  NOTE: There are no positions in the AF that are identified as drivers.

Identify Positional Support for Air Force GOs

- Executive officers (may be officers or civilians): any position satisfying one of the following conditions:
  - any AFSC title with "EXECUTIVE OFFICER" as part of it
  - any duty title exactly equal to "ASSISTANT EXECUTIVE", "EXECUTIVE OFFICER", "CXO", or "AXO"
  - any duty title with "EXECUTIVE OF", "EXEC OF", " XO", "XO ", "/XO", "XO,", "EXEC TO ", "EXECUTIVE TO ", or " EXECUTIVE TO" as part of it
  - any duty title exactly equal to "EXEC ASSISTANT", or "SR EXEC ASST", conditional on being a commissioned officer.

  <u>**Air Force Special Additions**</u>
  - Any duty title exactly equal to "PROGRAM EXECUTIVE OFFICER" not categorized as an executive officer.

- Administrative assistants (civilians only): any position satisfying one of the following conditions:
  - any AFSC or duty title with both "ADMIN" and "ASS" as part of it, conditional on being a civilian
  - any AFSC or duty title with both "EX" and "ASS" as part of it, conditional on being a civilian
  - any AFSC or duty title with "SECRETARY" or "SP ASST" as part of it
  - any AFSC or duty title exactly equal to "ASSISTANT", "ADMIN ASSISTANT", "ADMIN ASST", "SEC/CLERK/STENO", "OFF SPT ASST OA", "SEC-OFC AUTOMATING", "EXEC ASSISTANT", "SR EXEC ASST", or "EXEC ADMIN".

  <u>**Air Force Special Additions**</u>
  - Any AFSC whose first two elements include "3F", conditional on being a civilian.

- Executive assistants (enlisted only): any position satisfying one of the following conditions:
  - any AFSC title or duty title with "ADM ASST", "EXEC ASST", "ENL ASST", "PERS ASST", "CLERICAL ASST", "SEC TO ", or "ADM SUP" as part of it, conditional on being enlisted
  - any AFSC title or duty title with both "ADMIN" and "ASST" as part of it, conditional on being enlisted.

NOTE: None of these result in any matches for the Air Force.

Air Force Special Additions
- Any AFSC whose first two elements include "3F", conditional on being enlisted.

- Categorization corrections
  - A correction is applied to recategorize a commissioned officer as an "executive officer" if otherwise assigned as an "administrative assistant" or an "executive assistant."
  - A correction is applied to recategorize a civilian as an "administrative assistant" if otherwise assigned as an "executive assistant."
  - A correction is applied to recategorize an enlisted service member as an "executive assistant" if otherwise assigned as an "administrative assistant" or an "executive officer."
- Protocol: any position satisfying one of the following conditions:
  - any duty title with "PROTOCOL" as part of it
  - any AFSC title with "PROTOCOL" as part of it.

Air Force Special Additions
- Any office symbol code (OSC) exactly equal to "CCP", "CDP", "DSP ", or "HAFDSP".
- Any functional account code (FAC) exactly equal to "101100".

- CAGs: any position satisfying one of the following conditions:
  - any AFSC title or duty title with "ACTION", "WRITER", or "CAG" as part of it.

Air Force Special Additions
- Any OSC exactly equal to "A1I", "CCX", "CCXT", "CWDX", or "HAFDSX".
- Any FAC exactly equal to "11A600".

Associate Staff with an Air Force GO

In the Air Force, not all staff categorized as personal and positional staff are associated with a GO (they are instead associated with more-junior officers or other offices within that unit). We identify positions likely associated with providing personal or positional support to a GO in a UIC-OSC (e.g., FF04L0 CC) group as follows:[1]

1. Identify the highest rank within a UIC-OSC group.
2. Positions assigned to a unique UIC-OSC group whose highest rank is a GO will be treated as positional or personal staff categorized as above if they share the same UIC-OSC group.

---

[1] OSCs identify the organization structure and functional responsibilities within a unit.

3. For UIC-OSC groups with multiple GOs, we assign support staff to the highest-ranking GO first, then second, and so on.
   a. If the number of support staff exceed the number of GOs, then repeat by assigning the excess first to the highest GO, then to the second highest, and so on.
   b. Exception: Protocol and CAGs are associated with the highest-ranking GO in a UIC.

The CSAF is the only position assigned in his or her respective UIC. Similarly, the vice chief of staff of the Air Force has limited positions assigned to his or her UIC. In discussions with staff in the AF/A1, we determined that the support positions for these G/FOs were assigned to the unit affiliated with the director of the Air Staff. Additionally, another unit that provided support for the CSAF and Vice Chief of Staff of the Air Force was identified by staff in the AF/A1. Consequently, we affiliate all positions in these units with the CSAF's UIC.

B.2. Army GO Support Positions

We derived the Army sample from manning documents of units with at least one GO assigned in FY 2018 (units are identified by UIC). For the Army, manning documents reflect tables of organization extracted from the Army's Force Management System website. The study team collected these data.

Identify Personal Staff for Army GOs
- Aides-de-camp: any position satisfying one of the following conditions:
  - any position description with "AIDE DE CAMP", "AIDE-DE-CAMP", or "AIDE TO" as part of it
  - any position description exactly equal to "AIDE".
- Enlisted aides: identified by a separate file provided by OSD GOMO.
- Drivers/other personal support:[2] any position satisfying one of the following conditions:
  - any position description exactly equal to "ADMIN ASST/DRIVER" or "ENLISTED ASST/DRIVER".

---

[2] A service member assigned to a driver position may fulfill that role only part time. It is not possible to estimate the amount of time dedicated to driving the G/FO, but it is a necessary duty and overhead requirement, so they have been assessed as personal support staff. In a few cases, specifically in the Army, a G/FO may have two drivers: one for his assigned tactical vehicle in the field and one for nontactical vehicles in garrison.

Army Special Additions
– Any position description exactly equal to "VEHICLE DRIVER", or "DRIVER".

Identify Positional Support for Army GOs

- Executive officers (may be officers or civilians): any position satisfying one of the following conditions:
    – any position description with "EXECUTIVE OFFICER" as part of it
    – any position description exactly equal to "ASSISTANT EXECUTIVE", "EXECUTIVE OFFICER", "CXO", or "AXO"
    – any position description with "EXECUTIVE OF", "EXEC OF", " XO", "XO ", "/XO", "XO,", "EXEC TO ", "EXECUTIVE TO ", or " EXECUTIVE TO" as part of it
    – any position description exactly equal to "EXEC ASSISTANT", or "SR EXEC ASST", conditional on being an officer.

Army Special Additions
– Any position description with "XO" or " EXEC TO" as part of it.

- Administrative assistants (civilians only): any position satisfying one of the following conditions:
    – any position description with both "ADMIN" and "ASS" as part of it, conditional on being a civilian
    – any position description with both "EX" and "ASS" as part of it, conditional on being a civilian
    – any position description with "SECRETARY" or "SP ASST" as part of it
    – any position description exactly equal to "ASSISTANT", "ADMIN ASSISTANT", "ADMIN ASST", "SEC/CLERK/STENO", "OFF SPT ASST OA", "SEC-OFC AUTOMATING", "EXEC ASSISTANT", "SR EXEC ASST", or "EXEC ADMIN".

Army Special Additions
– Any position description with "ADMIN" and "SPEC" as part of it, conditional on being a civilian.
– Any position description with "ADMIN" and "OFF" as part of it, conditional on being a civilian.

- Executive assistants (enlisted only): any position satisfying one of the following conditions:
  - any position description with "ADM ASST", "EXEC ASST", "ENL ASST", "PERS ASST", "CLERICAL ASST", "SEC TO ", or "ADM SUP" as part of it, conditional on being enlisted
  - any position description with both "ADMIN" and "ASST" as part of it, conditional on being enlisted.

  Army Special Additions
  - Any position description with both "ADMIN" and "ASS" as part of it, conditional on being enlisted.
  - Any position description with both "EX" and "ASS" as part of it, conditional on being enlisted.
  - Any position description with "SP ASS" or "EXEC ADMIN" as part of it, conditional on being enlisted.

- Recategorization corrections
  - A correction is applied to recategorize a commissioned officer as an "executive officer" if otherwise assigned as an "administrative assistant" or an "executive assistant."
  - A correction is applied to recategorize a civilian as an "administrative assistant" if otherwise assigned as an "executive assistant."
  - A correction is applied to recategorize an enlisted service member as an "executive assistant" if otherwise assigned as an "administrative assistant" or an "executive officer."
- Protocol: any position satisfying one of the following conditions:
  - any position description with "PROTOCOL" as part of it.

  Army Special Additions
  - None.

- CAGs: any position satisfying one of the following conditions:
  - any position description with "ACTION", "WRITER", or "CAG" as part of it.

  Army Special Additions
  - Any position description with "STRATEGIC PLANNER" as part of it.
  - Any position description with both "STRAT" and "INIT" as part of it.
  - Any position description with both "STRAT" and "PLNR" as part of it.
  - Any position description with both "INIT" and "GR" as part of it.
  - Any position description with both "STRAT" and "STUD" as part of it.

Associate Staff with Army GOs

In the Army, not all staff categorized as personal and positional staff are associated with a GO (they are instead associated with more-junior officers or other offices within that unit). We identify positions likely associated with providing personal or positional support to a GO in a unit as follows:

1. Identify the highest grade within a UIC.
2. Positions assigned to a unique UIC whose highest grade is a GO will be treated as positional or personal staff categorized as above if they are within the same billet paragraph number (PARNO) as a GO.
3. For UIC PARNO groups with multiple G/FOs, we assign support staff to the highest-ranking GO first, then second, and so on.
   a. If the number of support staff exceed the number of GOs, then repeat by assigning the excess first to the highest GO, then to the second highest, and so on.
   b. Exception: Protocol and CAGs are associated with the highest-ranking GO with whom they share the same first two digits of a PARNO.

B.3. Marine Corps GO Support Positions

We derived the Marine Corps sample from manning documents of units with at least one GO assigned in FY 2018 (units are identified by UIC). For the Marines Corps, manning documents reflect tables of organization extracted from the Marine Corps Total Force Structure Management System. These data were provided by the operations branch of the Total Force Structure Division in the Office of the Deputy Commandant (CD&I).

Identify Personal Staff for Marine Corps GOs

- Aides-de-camp: any positions satisfying one of the following conditions:
  - any position description with "AIDE DE CAMP", "AIDE-DE-CAMP", or "AIDE TO" as part of it
  - any position description exactly equal to "AIDE".
- Enlisted aides: identified by a separate file provided by OSD GOMO.
- Drivers/other personal support: any positions satisfying one of the following conditions:
  - any position description exactly equal to "ADMIN ASST / DRIVER" or "ENLISTED ASST/DRIVER".

Marine Corps Special Additions
- Any position description with "DRIVER" or "VEHICLE OPERATOR".

Identify Positional Support for Marine Corps GOs

- Executive officers (may be officers or civilians): any positions satisfying one of the following conditions:
  - any position description with "EXECUTIVE OFFICER" as part of it
  - any position description exactly equal to "ASSISTANT EXECUTIVE", "EXECUTIVE OFFICER", "CXO", or "AXO"
  - any position description with "EXECUTIVE OF", "EXEC OF", " XO", "XO ", "/XO", "XO,", "EXEC TO", "EXECUTIVE TO ", or " EXECUTIVE TO" as part of it
  - any position description exactly equal to "EXEC ASSISTANT", or "SR EXEC ASST", conditional on being an officer.

Marine Corps Special Additions
- Any position description with "MILITARY SECRETARY", "MILITARY ASSISTANT", "(AIDE)", or " AIDE" as part of it, conditional on being an officer.
- Any position description with "ADMIN" and "OFFICER" as part of it, conditional on being a civilian or an officer.

- Administrative assistants (civilians only): any position satisfying one of the following conditions:
  - any position description with both "ADMIN" and "ASS" as part of it, conditional on being a civilian
  - any position description with both "EX" and "ASS" as part of it, conditional on being a civilian
  - any position description with "SECRETARY" or "SP ASST" as part of it
  - any position description exactly equal to "ASSISTANT", "ADMIN ASSISTANT", "ADMIN ASST", "SEC/CLERK/STENO", "OFF SPT ASST OA", "SEC-OFC AUTOMATING", "EXEC ASSISTANT", "SR EXEC ASST", or "EXEC ADMIN".

Marine Corps Special Additions
- Any position description with "ADMIN" and "SPEC" as part of it, conditional on being a civilian.
- Any position description with "ADMIN" and "COOR" as part of it, conditional on being a civilian.

– Remove any position categorized as an administrative assistant based on the above criteria if the position description is exactly equal to "SEXUAL ASSAULT RESPONSE COORDINATOR (SARC)".

- Executive assistants (enlisted only): any position satisfying one of the following conditions:
    – any position description with "ADM ASST", "EXEC ASST", "ENL ASST", "PERS ASST", "CLERICAL ASST", "SEC TO ", or "ADM SUP" as part of it, conditional on being enlisted
    – any position description with both "ADMIN" and "ASST" as part of it conditional on being enlisted.

Marine Corps Special Additions
– Any position description with both "ADMIN" and "ASS" as part of it, conditional on being enlisted.
– Any position description with both "EX" and "ASS" as part of it, conditional on being enlisted.
– Any position description with both "ADMIN" and "SPEC" as part of it, conditional on being enlisted.
– Any position description with "EXECUTIVE ASSISTANT", "SP ASS", "EXEC ADMIN", or " AIDE" as part of it, conditional on being enlisted.
– Any position description with exactly equal to "EXEC ASSISTANT", "SR EXEC ASST", "ADMIN CHIEF", "ADMIN CLERK", or "CLERK", conditional on being enlisted.
– Remove any position categorized as an administrative assistant based on the above criteria if the position description is exactly equal to "SEXUAL ASSAULT RESPONSE COORDINATOR (SARC)".

- Recategorization corrections
    – A correction is applied to recategorize a commissioned officer as an "executive officer" if otherwise assigned as an "administrative assistant" or an "executive assistant."
    – A correction is applied to recategorize a civilian as an "administrative assistant" if otherwise assigned as an "executive assistant."
    – A correction is applied to recategorize an enlisted service member as an "executive assistant" if otherwise assigned as an "administrative assistant" or an "executive officer."
    – A correction is applied to remove any position categorized as support staff if the position description includes both "STAFF" and "SEC" as part of it.
        ◦ This correction is applied to remove a unit's staff secretary, which generally supports the organization or the chief of staff rather than a GO.

- Protocol: any position satisfying one of the following conditions:
  - any position description with "PROTOCOL" as part of it.

  Marine Corps Special Additions
  - Any position whose office description includes "PROTOCOL" as part of it.

- CAG: any position satisfying one of the following conditions:
  - any position description with "ACTION", "WRITER", or "CAG" as part of it.

  Marine Corps Special Additions
  - Any position whose office description includes "STRATEGIC INITIATIVES GROUP".
  - Remove any position categorized as part of a "CAG" based on the position description including "ACTION" or "WRITER" as part of it, as it is overly broad.

Associate Staff with a Marine Corps GO

In the Marine Corps, not all staff categorized as personal and positional staff are associated with a GO (they are instead associated with more-junior officers or other offices within that unit). Marine Corps manning documents include separate records for subordinate offices within a unit. We created unique codes for these subordinate offices for each positional record in the manning documents, which we refer to as OFFICEID. We identify positions likely associated with providing personal or positional support to a GO in a unit as follows:

- Identify the highest rank within a UIC-OFFICEID.
- Designate positions assigned to a unique UIC-OFFICEID whose highest grade is a GO to be treated as positional or personal staff categorized as above.
- For UIC-OFFICEIDs with multiple GOs, we assign support staff to the highest-ranking GO first, then second, and so on.
  - If the number of support staff exceed the number of GOs, then repeat by assigning the excess first to the highest GO, then to the second highest, and so on.
  - Exception: Protocol and CAGs are associated with the highest-ranking GO in a unit regardless of position relative to a unit GO.

In reviewing the Marine Corps manning documents, it was noted that G/FO support staff were associated with other offices in the UIC (e.g., protocol might have its own office, or front office administrative staff might be placed in the chief of staff's office). In these cases, the OFFICEID of the applicable office was adjusted to correspond to the G/FO's OFFICEID.

B.4. Navy FO Support Positions

We derived the Navy sample from manning documents of units with at least one FO assigned at the end of FY 2018 (units are identified by UIC). For the Navy, manning documents reflect information extracted from the Navy Total Force Manpower Management System. These data were provided by the Office of Navy Flag Officer Management, Distribution and Development.

Identify Personal Staff for Navy FOs
- Aides-de-camp: any position satisfying one of the following conditions:
  - any position description with "AIDE DE CAMP", "AIDE-DE-CAMP", or "AIDE TO" as part of it
  - any position description exactly equal to "AIDE".
- Enlisted aides: identified by a separate file provided by OSD GOMO
- Drivers/other personal support: any position satisfying one of the following conditions:
  - any position description exactly equal to "ADMIN ASST/DRIVER" or "ENLISTED ASST/DRIVER".

Navy Special Additions
- Any position description with "DRIVER" as part of it.

Identify Positional Support for Navy FOs
- Executive officers (may be officers or civilians): any position satisfying one of the following conditions:
  - any position description with "EXECUTIVE OFFICER" as part of it
  - any position description exactly equal to "ASSISTANT EXECUTIVE", "EXECUTIVE OFFICER", "CXO", or "AXO"
  - any position description with "EXECUTIVE OF", "EXEC OF", " XO", "XO ", "/XO", "XO,", "EXEC TO ", "EXECUTIVE TO ", or " EXECUTIVE TO" as part of it
  - any position description exactly equal to "EXEC ASSISTANT", or "SR EXEC ASST", conditional on being an officer.

Navy Special Additions
- Any position description with "EXEC ASST", "EXECUTIVE ASST", "EXECUTIVE ASSISTANT", "ASST TO", or "FLAG SEC" as part of it, conditional on being an officer.

- Administrative assistants (civilians only): There were no civilians included in the Navy manning documents. This section is imputed based on the average number of civilian administrative assistants used by the other services.

- Executive assistants (enlisted only): any position satisfying one of the following conditions:
  - any position description with "ADM ASST", "EXEC ASST", "ENL ASST", "PERS ASST", "CLERICAL ASST", "SEC TO ", or "ADM SUP" as part of it, conditional on being enlisted
  - any position description with both "ADMIN" and "ASST" as part of it, conditional on being enlisted.

Navy Special Additions
- None.

- Recategorization corrections
  - A correction is applied to recategorize a commissioned officer as an "executive officer" if otherwise assigned as an "administrative assistant" or an "executive assistant."
  - A correction is applied to recategorize a civilian as an "administrative assistant" if otherwise assigned as an "executive assistant."
  - A correction is applied to recategorize an enlisted service member as an "executive assistant" if otherwise assigned as an "administrative assistant" or an "executive officer."
- Protocol: any position satisfying one of the following conditions:
  - any position description with "PROTOCOL" as part of it.

Navy Special Additions
- None.

- CAG: any position satisfying one of the following conditions:
  - any position description with "ACTION", "WRITER", or "CAG" as part of it.

Navy Special Additions
- None.

Associate Staff with a Navy FO

In the Navy, not all staff categorized as personal and positional staff are associated with an FO (they are instead associated with more junior officers or other offices within that unit). We identify positions likely associated with providing personal or positional support to an FO in a unit as follows:

- Identify the highest rank within a UIC.

- Designate positions assigned to a unique UIC whose highest rank is a GO to be treated as positional or personal staff categorized as above if they share the same first two digits of an FO's Billet Sequence Code (BSC-2).[3]
- For UIC BSC-2 groups with multiple FOs, we assign support staff to the highest-ranking FO first, then second, and so on.
  - If the number of support staff exceed the number of FOs, then repeat by assigning the excess first to the highest FO, then to the second highest, and so on.
  - Exception 1: Protocol and CAGs are associated with the highest-ranking FO in a unit regardless of BSC-2.
  - Exception 2: FO in BSC-2= "09" and UIC = "N00011" are separated by the first three digits of the BSC code rather than the first two digits.

B.5. Joint Duty Assigned G/FO's Support Positions

We derived the joint G/FO position sample from manning documents of units with at least one G/FO assigned at the end of FY 2018 (units are identified by DEPTID). For joint duty assignments, manning documents reflect information extracted from DMDC's Field Training Management System. These data were provided by DMDC in conjunction with Total Force Manpower and Resources Directorate in the Office of the Under Secretary of Defense for Personnel and Readiness.

Identify Personal Staff for Joint Duty G/FOs

- Aides-de-camp: any position satisfying one of the following conditions:
  - any position description with "AIDE DE CAMP", "AIDE-DE-CAMP", or "AIDE TO" as part of it
  - any position description exactly equal to "AIDE".

  #### Joint Duty Assignment Special Additions
  - Any position description with "AIDE" and officer (note that this was done here because the file was restricted only to G/FO header DEPTID).

- Enlisted aides: identified by a separate file provided by OSD GOMO.
- Drivers/other personal support: any position satisfying one of the following conditions:

---

[3] Navy billets make reference to a primary billet (denoted by the BSC and UIC following "TO" in the title). Consequently, positions with "TO" are the primary UICs, and "FM" are the secondary UICs. To the degree that the FO has staff in the secondary UIC that are supporting him/her, these are also associated with the FO in the primary UIC.

- Any position description exactly equal to "ADMIN ASST / DRIVER" or "ENLISTED ASST/DRIVER".

Joint Duty Assignment Special Additions
- Any position description with "DRIVER" or "VEHICLE OPERATOR".
- Any position description exactly equal to "PERSONAL SECURITY DETAIL", "SECURITY SPEC", "SECURITY SPECIALIST (PROT SVC)", "SPECIAL SECURITY ADMINISTRATOR", "TRAVEL COORDINATOR", "CDRS TRAVEL SPEC", or "TRAVEL & TRANSPORTATION SPEC".

NOTE: In some combatant command billets, security is assigned in the manning document rather than through the PPO, which is why we include security support here.

Identify Positional Support for Joint Duty G/FOs

- Executive officers (may be officers or civilians): any position satisfying one of the following conditions:
  - any position description with "EXECUTIVE OFFICER" as part of it
  - any position description exactly equal to "ASSISTANT EXECUTIVE", "EXECUTIVE OFFICER", "CXO", or "AXO"
  - any position description with "EXECUTIVE OF", "EXEC OF", " XO", "XO ", "/XO", "XO,", "EXEC TO", "EXECUTIVE TO ", " EXECUTIVE TO", "ASST TO", or "FLAG SEC" as part of it
  - any position description exactly equal to "EXEC ASSISTANT", "SR EXEC ASST", conditional on being a commissioned officer.

Joint Duty Assignment Special Additions
- Any position description with "EXEC ASSIST", "EA TO", " EA", "EA, ", or "MA " as part of it.
- Any position description exactly equal to "EXECUTIVE STAFF SPECIALIST", "EXEC", "CC EXECUTIVE SUPPORT".
- Any position description exactly equal to "EXEC ADVISOR", conditional on being a civilian.
- Any position description with "MIL" and "ASS" as part of it, conditional on being a commissioned officer.

- Administrative assistants (civilians only): any positions satisfying one of the following conditions:
  - any position description with both "ADMIN" and "ASS" as part of it
  - any position description with both "EX" and "ASS" as part of it
  - any position description with "SECRETARY" or "SP ASST" as part of it

– any position description exactly equal to "ASSISTANT", "ADMIN ASSISTANT", "ADMIN ASST", "SEC/CLERK/STENO", "OFF SPT ASST OA", "SEC-OFC AUTOMATING", "EXEC ASSISTANT", "SR EXEC ASST", or "EXEC ADMIN".

Joint Duty Assignment Special Additions

– Any position description with "ADMINISTRATIVE STAFF", "SUPPORT SPECIAL", "ADMIN MGMT SPC", "ADMIN SPT SPEC", "ADMINISTRATION SUPPORT", or "SEC TO" as part of it, conditional on being a civilian.
– Any position description exactly equal to "ADMINISTRATIVE OFFICER" or "EXEC ADMIN SPEC", conditional on being a civilian.

- Executive assistants (enlisted only): any position satisfying one of the following conditions:
  – any position description with "ADM ASST", "EXEC ASST", "ENL ASST", "PERS ASST", "CLERICAL ASST", "SEC TO ", or "ADM SUP" as part of it, conditional on being enlisted
  – any position description with both "ADMIN" and "ASST" as part of it, conditional on being enlisted.

Joint Duty Assignment Special Additions

– Any position description with both "ADMIN" and "ASS" as part of it, conditional on being enlisted.
– Any position description with "ADMIN", "YEOMAN", or "SEC TO" as part of it, conditional on being enlisted.
  ∘ A correction is used to omit position description "SPECIAL SECURITY ADMINISTRATOR", "RS ADMIN/MSG DISTR" from being recategorized as executive assistants.
– Any position description exactly equal to "EXECUTIVE SPT SVCS SPEC" or "EXEC SUPPORT MANAGER", conditional on being enlisted.

- Recategorization corrections
  – A correction is applied to recategorize a commissioned officer as an "executive officer" if otherwise assigned as an "administrative assistant" or an "executive assistant."
  – A correction is applied to recategorize a civilian as an "administrative assistant" if otherwise assigned as an "executive assistant."
  – A correction is applied to recategorize an enlisted service member as an "executive assistant" if otherwise assigned as an "administrative assistant" or an "executive officer."
- Protocol: any position satisfying one of the following conditions:

  - any position description with "PROTOCOL" as part of it.

Joint Duty Assignment Special Additions
  - Any position description with "ENGAGEMENT PLANNER" as part of it.

- CAGs: any position satisfying one of the following conditions:
  - any position description with "ACTION", "WRITER", or "CAG" as part of it.

Joint Duty Assignment Special Additions
  - Any position description with "SAG" or "STRATEGIC PLANNER" as part of it.
  - Any position description exactly equal to "STRATEGIC ANALYST", "STRATEGIST", or "STRATEGIST PLANNER".

Associate Staff with a Joint Duty G/FO

In joint duty assignment manning documents, not all staff categorized as personal and positional staff are associated with a G/FO (they are instead associated with more-junior officers or other offices within that unit). We identify positions likely associated with providing personal or positional support to a G/FO in a DEPTID as follows:

- Identify the highest rank within a ten-digit DEPTID.
- Designate positions assigned to a unique DEPTID whose highest rank is a GO to be treated as positional or personal staff categorized as above if they share the same DEPTID.
- For DEPTIDs with multiple G/FOs, we assign support staff to the highest-ranking G/FO first, then second, and so on.
  - If the number of support staff exceed the number of G/FOs, then repeat by assigning the excess first to the highest G/FO, then to the second highest, and so on.
  - Exception 1: Protocol and CAGs are associated with the highest-ranking G/FO in a DEPTID.

Some G/FO positions had support staff assigned to a slightly different DEPTID. For example, the commander of U.S. European Command is in DEPTID = "B00900000" and special assistants to the commander are in DEPTID = "B00900001B." Where identified, we have associated the office associated with these support staff (as represented by the DEPTID) with the G/FO position's office (as represented by the DEPTID). Specific G/FO positions where we did this include:

- commander, U.S. European Command and NATO Supreme Allied Commander, Europe
- commander, U.S. Strategic Command

- commander, U.S. Cyber Command
- commander, U.S. Central Command
- commander, USFOR-A, and NATO Commander, Resolute Support
- commander, U.S. Africa Command
- CJCS
- commander, U.S. Northern Command
- commander, U.S. Southern Command
- commander, U.S. Special Operations Command
- commander, U.S. Transportation Command
- commander, U.S. Indo-Pacific Command
- commander, USFK, and commander, Combined Forces Command
- director, Defense Information Security Agency
- director, Joint Staff
- director for Operations, J-3, Joint Staff
- director for Logistics, J-4, Joint Staff
- director, Strategic Plans and Policy, J-5, Joint Staff
- director for Operational Plans and Joint Force Development, J-7, Joint Staff
- director, Force Structure, Resources and Assessment, J-8, Joint Staff
- deputy commander, U.S. Indo-Pacific Command
- deputy commander, USFK, and commander, Combined Forces Command.

References

Asch, Beth J., James Hosek, Jennifer Kavanagh, and Michael G. Mattock, *Retention, Incentives, and DoD Experience Under the 40-Year Military Pay Table*, Santa Monica, Calif.: RAND Corporation, RR-1209-OSD, 2016. As of October 10, 2019:
https://www.rand.org/pubs/research_reports/RR1209.html

Chairman of the Joint Chiefs of Staff Instruction 1801.01D, *National Defense University Policy*, June 10, 2015. As of October 10, 2019:
https://www.jcs.mil/Portals/36/Documents/Library/Instructions/1801_01.
pdf?ver=2016-02-05-175010-047

Chandrasekaran, Rajiv, and Greg Jaffe, "Petraeus Scandal Puts Four-Star General Lifestyle Under Scrutiny," *Washington Post*, November 17, 2012. As of October 10, 2019:
https://www.washingtonpost.com/world/national-security/petraeus-scandal-puts-four-star-general-lifestyle-under-scrutiny/2012/11/17/33a14f48-3043-11e2-a30e-5ca76eeec857_story.html

Defense Manpower Data Center, "Department of Defense Active Duty Military Personnel by Rank/Grade (Updated Monthly)," Alexandria, Va.: U.S. Department of Defense, September 2001–2018 and May 2019. As of October 10, 2019:
https://www.dmdc.osd.mil/appj/dwp/dwp_reports.jsp

Defense Travel Management Office, "Basic Allowance for Housing (BAH)," webpage, Washington D.C.: U.S. Department of Defense, 2019a. As of August 9, 2019:
https://www.defensetravel.dod.mil/site/bah.cfm

Defense Travel Management Office, "Overseas Allowance for Housing (OHA)," webpage, Washington D.C.: Department of Defense, 2019b. As of August 9, 2019:
https://www.defensetravel.dod.mil/site/oha.cfm

Department of Defense Directive 4500.56, *DoD Policy on the Use of Government Aircraft and Air Travel*, Washington, D.C.: U.S. Department of Defense, April 14, 2009, Incorporating Change 5, Effective April 3, 2019. As of August 9, 2019:
https://www.esd.whs.mil/Portals/54/Documents/DD/issuances/dodd/450056p.
pdf?ver=2019-04-03-081124-490

Department of Defense Instruction 1315.09, *Utilization of Enlisted Aides (EAs) on Personal Staffs of General and Flag Officers (GO/FOs)*, Washington D.C.: U.S. Department of Defense, March 6, 2015, Incorporating Change 1, December 1, 2017. As of October 10, 2019:
https://www.esd.whs.mil/Portals/54/Documents/DD/issuances/dodi/131509p.
pdf?ver=2017-12-01-105430-597

Department of Defense Instruction 7250.13, *Use of Appropriated Funds for Official Representation Purposes*, Washington D.C.: U.S. Department of Defense, June 30, 2009, Incorporating Change 1, Effective September 17, 2017. As of October 10, 2019:
https://www.esd.whs.mil/Portals/54/Documents/DD/issuances/dodi/725013p.pdf?ver=2019-04-04-075543-010

Department of Defense Instruction O-2000.22A, *Designation and Physical Protection of DoD High-Risk Personnel*, Washington D.C.: U.S. Department of Defense, June 19, 2014. As of October 10, 2019:
https://directives.whs.mil/issuances/O200022p.pdf (access restricted)

Department of Defense Manual 4165.63, *DoD Housing Management*, Washington, D.C.: U.S. Department of Defense, October 28, 2010, Incorporating Change 2, August 31, 2018. As of October 10, 2019:
https://www.esd.whs.mil/Portals/54/Documents/DD/issuances/dodm/416563m.pdf

DMDC—*See* Defense Manpower Data Center.

DoDI—*See* Department of Defense Instruction.

DoDIG—*See* Office of the Inspector General, Department of Defense.

DTMO—*See* Defense Travel Management Office.

GAO—*See* U.S. Government Accountability Office.

Harrington, Lisa M., Bart E. Bennett, Katharina Ley Best, David R. Frelinger, Paul W. Mayberry, Igor Mikolic-Torreira, Sebastian Joon Bae, Barbara Bicksler, Lisa Davis, Steven Deane-Shinbrot, Joslyn Fleming, Benjamin Goirigolzarri, Russell Hanson, Connor P. Jackson, Kimberly Jackson, Sean Mann, Geoffrey McGovern, Jenny Oberholtzer, Christina Panis, Alexander D. Rothenberg, Ricardo Sanchez, Matthew Sargent, Peter Schirmer, Hilary Reininger, and Mitch Tuller, *Realigning the Stars: A Methodology for Reviewing Active Component General and Flag Officer Requirements*, Santa Monica, Calif.: RAND Corporation, RR-2384-OSD, 2018. As of July 18, 2019:
https://www.rand.org/pubs/research_reports/RR2384.html

Hosek, James, Beth J. Asch, and Michael G. Mattock, *Toward Efficient Military Retirement Accrual Charges*, Santa Monica, Calif.: RAND Corporation, RR-1373-A, 2017. As of July 18, 2019:
https://www.rand.org/pubs/research_reports/RR1373.html

Hosek, James, Beth J. Asch, Michael G. Mattock, and Troy D. Smith, *Military and Civilian Pay Levels, Trends, and Recruit Quality*, Santa Monica, Calif.: RAND Corporation, RR-2396-OSD, 2018. As of July 18, 2019:
https://www.rand.org/pubs/research_reports/RR2396.html

Kamarck, Kristy N., *Concurrent Receipt: Background and Issues for Congress*, Washington D.C.: Congressional Research Service, R40589, January 17, 2019. As of August 9, 2019:
https://fas.org/sgp/crs/misc/R40589.pdf

McAndrew, Anne, *Fiscal Year (FY) 2019 Department of Defense (DoD) Civilian Personnel Fringe Benefit Rates*, Washington, D.C.: U.S. Department of Defense, October 1, 2018. As of August 9, 2019:
https://comptroller.defense.gov/Portals/45/documents/rates/fy2019/2019_d.pdf

Offenhauer, Priscilla, *General and Flag Officer Authorizations for the Active and Reserve Components: A Comparative and Historical Analysis*, Washington, D.C.: Library of Congress, Federal Research Division, December 2007. As of July 18, 2019:
http://www.loc.gov/rr/frd/pdf-files/CNGR_General-Flag-Officer-Authorizations.pdf

Office of Personnel Management, "General Schedule Classification and Pay," webpage, Washington D.C., undated. As of August 9, 2019:
https://www.opm.gov/policy-data-oversight/pay-leave/pay-systems/general-schedule/

Office of the Inspector General, Department of Defense, *Audit Report: Maintenance and Repair of DoD General and Flag Officer Quarters*, Arlington, Va., Report No. D-2000-071, January 27, 2000. As of July 18, 2019:
https://media.defense.gov/2000/Jan/27/2001715710/-1/-1/1/00-071.pdf

Office of the Inspector General, Department of Defense, *Report of Investigation: Rick A. Uribe, Brigadier General, U.S. Marine Corps*, Arlington, Va., Report No. DODIG-2018-131, June 14, 2018. As of October 28, 2019:
https://media.defense.gov/2018/Jul/10/2001940716/-1/-1/1/DODIG-2018-131%20UPDATED%202.PDF

Office of the Secretary of Defense, Office of Cost Assessment and Program Evaluation, "FCOM Military Rates 2016: White Paper—References, Calculations, and Assumptions," Washington, D.C.: U.S. Department of Defense, August 2017a.

Office of the Secretary of Defense, Office of Cost Assessment and Program Evaluation, *Defining General and Flag Officer Costs*, Washington, D.C.: U.S. Department of Defense, December 2017b.

Office of the Secretary of Defense, Office of Cost Assessment and Program Evaluation, "FCOM Civilian Rates 2019: White Paper—References and Calculations," Washington, D.C.: U.S. Department of Defense, May 2019.

OPM—*See* Office of Personnel and Management.

OSD, CAPE—*See* Office of the Secretary of Defense, Office of Cost Assessment and Program Evaluation.

Public Law 114-92, National Defense Authorization Act for Fiscal Year 2016, November 25, 2015.

Public Law 115-232, John S. McCain National Defense Authorization Act for Fiscal Year 2019, August 13, 2018.

Rosen, Sherwin, "The Military as an Internal Labor Market: Some Allocative, Productivity, and Incentive Problems," *Social Science Quarterly*, Vol. 73, No. 2, June 1992, pp. 49–64.

Seacord, James M., *Adjusted 2019 Defense Civilian Intelligence Personnel System Pay Rates*, Washington, D.C.: U.S. Department of Defense, Office of the Under Secretary of Defense, April 2, 2019. As of August 9, 2019:
https://dcips.defense.gov/Portals/50/Documents/Adjusted%202019%20DCIPS%20Pay%20Rates%20&%20Ranges%20(Final%20Signed).pdf

Tompkey, Mary E., *FY 2019 Department of Defense (DoD) Military Personnel Composite Standard Pay and Reimbursement Rates*, Washington, D.C.: U.S. Department of Defense, Office of the Under Secretary of Defense, March 30, 2018. As of August 9, 2019:
https://comptroller.defense.gov/Portals/45/documents/rates/fy2019/2019_k.pdf

U.S. Code, Title 10, Section 525, Distribution of Commissioned Officers on Active Duty in General Office and Flag Officer Grades. As of October 16, 2019:
https://www.law.cornell.edu/uscode/text/10/525

U.S. Code, Title 10, Section 526, Authorized Strength: General and Flag Offices on Active Duty. As of October 16, 2019:
https://www.law.cornell.edu/uscode/text/10/526

U.S. Code, Title 10, Section 526a, Authorized Strength After December 31, 2022: General Officers and Flag Officers on Active Duty. As of October 16, 2019:
https://www.law.cornell.edu/uscode/text/10/526a

U.S. Code, Title 10, Section 981, Limitation on Number of Enlisted Aides. As of December 12, 2019:
https://www.law.cornell.edu/uscode/text/10/981

U.S. Department of Defense, "Military Compensation: Basic Allowance for Subsistence (BAS)," webpage, undated-a. As of August 9, 2019:
https://militarypay.defense.gov/Pay/Allowances/BAS.aspx

U.S. Department of Defense, "Military Compensation: Regular Military Compensation (RMC) Calculator," webpage, undated-b. As of August 9, 2019:
https://militarypay.defense.gov/Calculators/RMC-Calculator/

U.S. General Accounting Office, *Report to Congress: Enlisted Aide Program of the Military Services*, Washington, D.C.: Comptroller General of the United States, B-177516, April 18, 1973. As of July 18, 2019:
https://www.gao.gov/products/096396

U.S. General Accounting Office, *DoD Use of Official Representation Fund to Entertain Foreign Dignitaries*, report to the Comptroller General, report to the ranking minority member, Committee on Government Operations House of Representatives of the United States, Washington, D.C., GAO/ID-83-7, December 29, 1982. As of July 18, 2019:
https://www.gao.gov/products/GAO/ID-83-7

U.S. General Accounting Office, *Information on the Military Services' Enlisted Aide Program*, Washington, D.C.: National Security and International Affairs Division, B-207788, October 11, 1983. As of July 18, 2019:
https://www.gao.gov/products/NSIAD-84-12

U.S. Government Accountability Office, *Military Personnel: Military and Civilian Pay Comparisons Present Challenges and Are One of Many Tools in Assessing Compensation*, Washington, D.C., GAO-10-561R, April 2010. As of October 10, 2019:
https://www.gao.gov/assets/100/96645.pdf

U.S. Government Accountability Office, *Human Capital: Opportunities Exist to Further Improve DOD's Methodology for Estimating the Costs of Its Workforces*, Washington, D.C., GAO-13-792, September 2013. As of July 18, 2019:
https://www.gao.gov/assets/660/658131.pdf

U.S. Government Accountability Office, *Military Personnel: DOD Needs to Update General and Flag Officer Requirements and Improve Availability of Associated Costs*, Washington, D.C., GAO-14-745, September 2014. As of October 10, 2019:
https://www.gao.gov/assets/670/665651.pdf

U.S. Government Accountability Office, *Military Enlisted Aides: DOD's Report Met Most Statutory Requirements, but Aide Allocation Could Be Improved*, Washington, D.C., GAO-16-239, February 22, 2016. As of July 18, 2019:
https://www.gao.gov/products/GAO-16-239